AF016

MASSIMILIANO AFIERO

AXIS FORCES 16

WW2 AXIS FORCES

The Axis Forces 016 - First edition December 2020 by Luca Cristini Editor for the brand Soldiershop
Cover & Art Design by soldiershop factory. ISBN code: 978-88-93276948
Copyright © 2020 Luca Cristini Editore (BG) ITALY. No part of this publication may be reproduced, stored in a retrieval system or transmitted by any form or by any means, electronic, recording or otherwise without the prior permission in writing from the publishers. The publisher remains to disposition of the possible having right for all the doubtful sources images or not identifies. Visit www.soldiershop.com to read more about all our books and to buy them.

The Axis Forces number 16 – December 2020

Direction and editing
Via San Giorgio, 11 – 80021 AFRAGOLA (NA) -ITALY
Managing and Chief Editor: Massimiliano Afiero
Email: maxafiero@libero.it - **Website**: www.maxafiero.it

Contributors
Tomasz Borowski, Grégory Bouysse, Stefano Canavassi, Carlos Caballero Jurado, Rene Chavez, Gary Costello, Paolo Crippa, Carlo Cucut, Antonio Guerra, John B. Köser, Lars Larsen, Christophe Leguérandais, Eduardo M. Gil Martínez, Michael D. Miller, Peter Mooney, Péter Mujzer, Ken Niewiarowicz, Erik Norling, Raphael Riccio, Marc Rikmenspoel, Samcevich Andrei, Charles Trang, Cesare Veronesi, Sergio Volpe

Editorial

Hi guys. Here we are again to talk about past history, during a present that is difficult to face the past, with a present that is difficult to face and a future still uncertain due to this pandemic that does not want to leave us. It is very difficult to continue working in this apocalyptic climate, but we all have to convince ourselves to return to normal as soon as possible, then resume our historical research but above all, return to life. Closed within the home to limit infections and the spread of the pandemic, we have at least had more time to explore new topics and new themes to try to improve the level of our articles and our magazine, especially to meet the needs of our readers. scattered all over the world. However, our invitation to you all to continue to report new topics and themes of your choice on which to write new articles for the next issues of our magazine remains valid. Waiting for your comments and your suggestions, let's now analyze the contents of this new issue: let's start with the use of the SS cavalry units on the Polish front between 1939 and 1941, mainly engaged as security forces and in the anti-partisan struggle. Following is the biography of Herbert-Otto Gille, one of the most representative figures of the Waffen-SS, regimental, division and army corps commander. We continue with the fourth part of the article dedicated to the employment of the Cossacks in the German armed forces. Let's go back to talking about the units of the Italian Social Republic, in particular the armored group Leonessa, an article accompanied by many unpublished photos. We conclude with a new article dedicated to German anti-tank weapons, talking about anti-tank rifles. Happy reading to all and see you next issue.

Massimiliano Afiero

The publication of The Axis Forces deals exclusively with subjects of a historical military nature and is not intended to promote any type of political ideology either present or past, as it also does not seek to exalt any type of political regime of the past century or any form of racism.

Contents

The SS cavalry units in Poland, 1939-1941	Pag. 5
General der Waffen-SS Herbert Otto Gille	Pag. 16
Hitler's Cossacks part 4	Pag. 40
The Tankers of Mussolini - R.S.I.'s "M" Armored Group "Leonessa"	Pag. 51
German Antitank Rifles in WW2	Pag. 65

The Axis Forces

in World War Two 1939-1945

The SS cavalry units in Poland, 1939-1941
by Massimiliano Afiero

Hermann Fegelein in the *Allgemeine-SS* uniform, 1939.

SS-Stubaf. Franz Magill.

The Berittene Abteilung

On September 15, 1939, while the Polish campaign was still under way, Himmler ordered the formation of the first cavalry unit (*Berittene Abteilung*, horse-mounted unit) within the *SS-Totenkopfverbande*, for use in the recently conquered territories. This unit, under the command of *SS-Staf.* Fegelein, was formed in Berlin and consisted of a staff (*Stab*), and four squadrons, numbered 1 through 4. Most of the personnel came from the *SS-Reiter-Standarten* of the *Allgemeine-SS*, with some cadre also coming from the *Schutzpolizei*.

1.Schwadron, *SS-Stubaf.* Franz Magill
2.Schwadron, *SS-Ostuf.* Herbert Schönfeldt
3.Schwadron, *SS-Stubaf.* Rudolf Ruge
4.Schwadron, *SS-Hstuf.* Rolf Becher

When its formation was completed, the *Berittene Abteilung* consisted of 27 officers, 424 men and 399 horses. It was also decided that the formation of additional squadrons would be carried out directly in Poland. Training was thus reduced to a minimum from the time that transfer to the Polish front began on September 21. Initially the staff and *1.Schwadron* were transferred to Posen, which was to serve as a temporary base. 2. and *3.Schwadronen* were also moved to Posen, in the ex-*Königs-Jägerkaserne*, while *4.Schwadron* was billeted at Lucmierz, thirteen kilometers north of Łódź. By Himmler's order, the entire unit was subordinated to *HSSuPF* "Ost" (*Höherer SS und Polizeiführer*, the High Commander of the SS and Police) *SS-Obergruppenführer* Friedrich Wilhelm Krüger, who was also to be responsible for its expansion.

The Axis Forces

Polish civilians captured by German cavalry units.

An SS cavalry unit in Poland, September 1939.

Polish civilians, captured by German soldiers, 1939.

Early operations

The *Berittene Abteilung* was supposed to be used as a second-line unit in police operations and above all in sweeps in occupied territories. The sweeps consisted of searching for groups of isolated Polish soldiers who had been bypassed by the rapid advance of German troops and who had been completely cut off from their former headquarters. These groups of surviving units constituted a potential threat to foster the formation of partisan bands acting against the occupation forces. The SS missions also included the search for and confiscation of all weapons still in the hands of the Polish populace, protection of the *Volksdeutschen* (the German population residing in Polish territory) from possible reprisals by the Poles, and deportation of the Polish population to work camps in Germany or within the General Government of Poland itself, and the capture of common criminals who had escaped from jail during the confusion following the fighting. Overall the main activity was to restore order following the anarchy resulting from the dissolution of Polish institutions. Polish guerrilla resistance, which was attempting to organize, was destroyed in its infancy decisively and remorselessly. The methods used by the Germans were simple and extreme: anyone who broke German or Polish laws was deported to a work camp. Anyone who tried to resist or escape was shot on the spot. The *Berittene Abteilung* operated in conjunction with other second-line German units, as well as with the Polish police. On September 27, *1.* and *4.Schwadron* began a series of operations.

The Axis Forces

Waldemar Fegelein in 1937.

1.Schwadron was engaged in maintaining control over the highway between Łodź and Zgierz and the cities of Kaly and Anderejow. Meanwhile *4.Schwadron* sent out four patrols, each with the strength of half a platoon, to clear the cities of Orla, Grodnici and the forests between Krasnodeby and Grodnici. From there they moved on Bzura, Ruta, Alexandrow, Jastrzebia, Bruzyczka and Piaskowice. During these sweeps, many Polish soldiers were captured and large quantities of arms and ammunition were seized. The two squadrons continued their activities into the month of October, always meeting with excellent results.

SS-Totenkopf-Reiter-Standarte

On November 15, 1939, by order of Krüger, the unit was officially renamed as the *SS-Totenkopf-Reiter-Standarte*. During the same period, per Himmler's orders, it was decided to increase the unit to twelve squadrons and it was also decided to form a reserve unit at the *SS-Hauptreitschule* of Munich. The various units of the *SS-Totenkopf-Reiter-Standarte* were billeted in the following locations:

Unit	Location	Commander
Stab	Warsaw	Commander: *SS-Staf.* Hermann Fegelein Ia: *SS-Stubaf.* Günther Temme
1.*Schwadron*	Warsaw	*SS-Hstuf.* Waldemar Fegelein
2.*Schwadron*	Garwolin	*SS-Stubaf.* Rudolf Ruge
3.*Schwadron*	Seroczyn	*SS-Hstuf.* Gustav Lombard
4.*Schwadron*	Zamosc	*SS-Stubaf.* Josef Fritz
5.*Schwadron*	Chelm	*SS-Hstuf.* Wilhelm Reichenwallner
6.*Schwadron*	Tarnow	*SS-Hstuf.* Hans-Viktor von Zastrow
7.*Schwadron*	Krakow	*SS-Ostuf.* Herbert Schönfeldt
8.*Schwadron*	Kielce	*SS-Hstuf.* Walter Dunsch
9.(Ersatz) *Schwadon*	Munich	*SS-Ostuf.* Karl Fritsche
10.(schw.) *Schwadron*	Kamienna	*SS-Ostuf.* Franz Rinner
11.(Tec.) *Schwadron*	Lublin	*SS-Stubaf.* Franz Magill
12. *Reiter-Batterie*	Krakow	*Oberleutnant der Schutzpolizei* Arno Paul
Sanitätsstaffel	Warsaw	*SS-Ostuf.* Dr. Harald Strohschneider

German soldiers executing Polish civilians.

The stationing of the various squadrons over such a vast territory naturally caused problems of liaison between them, especially during the winter season. With the deterioration of weather conditions, and with the roads becoming impassable, partisan bands intensified their activity, putting a heavy burden on the SS cavalry units. In the Seroczyn sector, for example, *3.Schwadron* was engaged for several weeks against a number of partisan groups. *1.Schwadron* had to detach some platoons to execute hundreds of Polish civilians during sweep operations. *5.Schwadron* was also used to execute hundreds of other Polish prisoners guilty of having attempted to escape during a transfer march from Chelm to Sokal. On December 15, 1939, Himmler ordered the unit to officially assume the name of *1.SS-Totenkopf-Reiterstandarte*.

Two photos of *SS-Staf.* Fegelein and Governor Hans Frank in Warsaw, December 1939.

At that time, the unit numbered 46 officers, 91 NCOs and 450 men. This new designation served to differentiate the unit from other cavalry units of the *Allgemeine-SS* but also indicated, by using the number 1, the desire to form other such units in the immediate future. Development of the regiment proceeded throughout the winter. The twelve planned squadrons were not completed until the summer of 1940, recruiting experienced cadre and personnel coming from already existing units, but replacements from Germany as well. In early 1940 the SS cavalry units continued to be assigned to operations for the maintenance of order and to operations against partisan bands. At the same time the training of new units continued and the search for horses to equip them also went ahead. Most of the animals were procured from Polish trainers as well as from circuses.

SS-Hstuf. Gustav Lombard in Poland, Spring 1940 (Charles Trang Collection).

Horses for SS cavalry unit (C. Trang).

The horses, most of which were sick and flea-ridden, were integrated into the squadrons after about a month, after having been treated by the regiment's veterinarians, led by *SS-Hstuf.* Hans Herling. Despite these difficulties, the new units were gradually formed, and the first inspections began on March 19, 1940; the first squadron was inspected by *SS-Obergruppenführer* August Heissmeyer, who at the time was in charge of the *SS-Hauptamt*.

The forests of Kamienna

On March 30, the *1.SS-Totenkopf-Reiterstandarte* was engaged for the first time in a large-scale anti-partisan operation. The unit was put on alert at 22:00 and a few minutes later, *SS-Obergruppenführer* Krüger ordered all of the units stationed in Krakow to march on Kielce. Once they had arrived there, *1.SS-Totenkopf-Reiterstandarte* received orders to send all available forces to the area of Skarzysko-Kamienna, where *10.Schwadron* set up its headquarters.

SS-Ogruf. Krüger.

An SS cavalry unit in Poland, March 1940 (*C. Trang Collection*).

SS Artillery forward observers, Poland 1940.

The bulk of the regiment reached the area the next day, in the late afternoon. The objective was to hold back and wipe out a band of Polish irregular soldiers, some three hundred, led by a captain, which had been spotted in the forest of Kamienna. For the operation the regiment engaged the 1st, 7th, 8th, 9th, 10th and 12th squadrons. These were supported by the *51.Polizei-Bataillon* of the *Ordnungspolizei* and by other security units. The cavalry units, along with the police, attacked on April 1, with the support of artillery belonging to *10.Schwadron*.

Threatened with being surrounded, the Polish *"irregulars"* attempted to escape from the enemy's grip, passing through the positions of the *51.Polizei-Bataillon* and initiating fighting that lasted several hours. The cavalrymen of *10.Schwadron* finally had to come to the aid of the German policemen; the Poles were forced to fall back towards Lomzna and the swamps of the Kamienna forest. Sweeps of villages in the area quickly followed; all adult males were either executed or deported, and the women and children were evacuated. It was not until 8 April that the partisan band was again surrounded and wiped out completely. Despite this success, the sweep operations continued for some days, directed against new villages, where deportations and mass executions continued.

German troops attacking enemies forces in a Polish forest, Spring 1940.

A SS German cavalry unit engaged in a sweep (*Trang*).

New units

At the beginning of May 1940, the *13.Schwadron* (partly motorized) and the *14.Schwadron* were formed, respectively in Warsaw and Krasnystaw, thanks to the influx of new recruits from the *Allgemeine-SS*. At the same time, the *Ersatz-Schwadron* from Munich was reduced to a single platoon while *9.(Ersatz) Schwadron* was transferred from Warsaw to Lucmierz. Around the middle of May, strength rose to a total of 1,908 men. On May 15, following the arrival of the recruits, it was decided to split the regiment into two distinct units, designated *1.* and *2.SS-Totenkopf-Reiterstandarten*. *1.SS-Totenkopf-Reiterstandarte*, commanded by *SS-Staf.* Hermann Fegelein, consisted of a headquarters (in Warsaw) with a signals platoon, a motorcycle platoon, an engineer platoon and a band. *2.SS-Totenkopf-Reiterstandarte*, commanded by *SS-Stubaf*. Franz Magill, consisted of a headquarters in Lublin with a signals platoon, a motorcycle platoon, an engineer platoon and a band. The other squadrons not used for the formation of the new regiments were disbanded and their personnel were used to strengthen the existing units. On June 1, 1940, the ex-*9.(Ersatz) Schwadron* was transformed into a new depot unit for both of the regiments along with the base unit from the *SS-Hauptreitschule* in Munich.

An SS cavalry unit in Krakow, 1940.

Horses for SS unit, 1940.

SS horsemen during an anti-partisan operation, 1940.

While there were no problems in recruiting new personnel, with respect to weapons and equipment sufficient quantities were lacking and quality was poor. Most of the equipment came from Polish and Czech warehouses, while the German equipment dated back to the First World War. The instructors nevertheless made great efforts to render all of the squadrons operational. The "police" missions nonetheless continued to keep the various cavalry squadrons very busy. The SS horsemen were engaged mainly in preventing fighting between the Polish and Ukrainian populace, who were always at odds. During the month of June, several squadrons were engaged in protecting the *Volksdeutschen* in Turek while at the same time ensuring the roundup of the Jewish population prior to their transfer to concentration camps. During the month of July, the Germans intensified the transfer of Poles to the east and to work camps, to ensure the transfer of *Volksdeutschen* and the Germans of Volinia to the evacuated territories. In the meantime, towards the end of July, the recruitment period for *2.SS-Totenkopf-*

Reiterstandarte was completed. On July 28, *1.SS-Totenkopf-Reiterstandarte* could muster 54 officers, 190 NCOs and 1,585 soldiers. *2.SS-Totenkopf-Reiterstandarte* had 31 officers, 114 NCOs and 1,366 soldiers. In September, 200 new recruits arrived from Munich. At the same time, members more than 35 years old were demobilized and sent back to Germany.

SS cavalry units drawn up for an official ceremony, Warsaw 1940.

SS cavalry units in training, Autumn 1940.

Also during the month of September, the SS horsemen were engaged in new *"police"* operations. Between September 19-20, *1.* and *5.Schwadron* of *1.SS-Tot.Reit.* arrested more than 1,600 Poles in Warsaw after a member of the SD (*Sicherheitsdienst*, the SS security service) was killed in an ambush.

New reorganization

On 11 November 1940, *SS-Obergruppenführer* Krüger inspected the two regiments while they were training and was very impressed by the performance of the SS cavalrymen. As a result of the report he sent to the *SS-Hauptamt*, it was decided to reunite the two regiments into a larger unit. On December 6, the *SS-FHA* thus consolidated the two *SS-Totenkopf-Reiterstandarten* into a single regiment, which in turn consisted of two half-regiments with two battalions each, designated as *SS-Totenkopf-Kavallerie-Regiment 1*. The term *Standarte* was thus replaced by a more military designation, which at that time applied to most of the *Waffen-SS* formations. Nonetheless, the new unit was not subordinate to the *Wehrmacht*, but remained at the disposition of the *Reichsführer-SS*.

SS-Totenkopf-Kavallerie-Regiment 1

Rgt.Kdr.: *SS-Staf.* Fegelein

1.Halb-Regiment (*SS-Staf.* Fegelein)

    I.Bataillon (Warsaw): *SS-Hstuf.* Gustav Lombard
    1.*Schwadron* (Warsaw): *SS-Hstuf.* W. Fegelein
    2.*Schwadron* (Garwolin): *SS-Hstuf.* Ulrich Görtz
    3.*Schwadron* (Warsaw): *SS-Ostuf.* Ernst Imhoff
    4.*Schwadron* (Jablon): *SS-Hstuf.* Meistrknecht
    5.*(MG)Schw.* (Lapiguz): *SS-Ostuf.* Gadischke

    II.Bataillon (Warsaw): *SS-Hstuf.* A. Fassbender
    6.*(Tec.) Schwadron*(*) (Warsaw): *SS-Ostuf.* Fritsche
    7.*Bttr.* (Warsaw): *SS-Hstuf.* Arno Paul
    8.*Aufkl.-Schwadron*(**) (Warsaw): *SS-Ostuf.* Plänk
    9.*(IG) Schwadron* (Warsaw): *SS-Ostuf.* Kotthaus
    Leichte Kolonne (mot.) (Seroczyn): *SS-Ostuf.* Peters

SS-Staf. **Hermann Fegelein.**

2.Halb-Regiment (*SS-Stubaf.* Magill)

    III.Bataillon (Krakow): *SS-Hstuf.* H. Schönfeldt
    1.*Schwadron* (Krakow): *SS-Ostuf.* Karl Zilling
    2.*Schwadron* (Kielce): *SS-Hstuf.* Walter Dunsch
    3.*Schwadron* (Tarnow): *SS-Hstuf.* von Zastrow
    4.*Schwadron* (Chelm): *SS-Hstuf.* Reichenwallner
    5.*(MG) Schwadron* (Zamosc): *SS-Ostuf.* Wegener

    IV.Bataillon (Lublin): *SS-Stubaf.* Magill
    6.*(Tec.) Schwadron*(*) (Lublin) : SS-Ustuf. Maletta
    7.*Bttr.* (Lublin): *SS-Ostuf.* Paul Hoppe
    8.*Aufkl.-Schw.*(**) (Lublin): *SS-Hstuf.* Lindemann
    9.*(IG) Schw.* (Lublin): *SS-Ustuf.* Hohenberger
    Leichte Kolonne (mot.) (Lublin): *SS-Ostuf.* Lange

SS-Hstuf. **Albert Fassbender.**

(*) Consisting of an engineer platoon, a signals platoon and an anti-tank platoon.
(**) Cyclist units.

Two squadrons, one based at the *SS-Unterführerschule* at Lucmierz and the other at the SS-Hauptreitschule in Munich, consinued to serve as depot units. This new unit structure was somewhat anomalous and reflected hesitation on the part of the *SS-FHA*, whose initial intention was to consolidate the two regiments into a brigade that was largely motorized and which had more firepower. In February 1941, the term *Totenkopf* and the half-regiment concept were abandoned and the two regiments were reorganized as *SS-Kavallerie-Regimenter 1* and *2*. They were to become operational by April 1.

SS-Ostuf. **Gustav Lombard.**

SS-Kavallerie-Regiment 1: *SS-Staf.* Hermann Fegelein
    Reitende Abteilung: *SS-Hstuf.* G. Lombard
    1.Schwadron: *SS-Hstuf.* Waldemar Fegelein
    2.Schwadron: *SS-Hstuf.* Ulrich Görtz
    3.Schwadron: *SS-Ostuf.* Johann Schmid
    4.(MG) Schwadron: *SS-Ostuf.* H. Gadischke
    5.(IG) Schwadron: *SS-Ostuf.* Siegfried Kotthaus
    6.(Tec.) Schwadron: *SS-Hstuf.* A. Fassbender
    7.(Radfahr/Aufkl)Schwadron: *SS-Ostuf.* Plänk
    8.reit.Bttr. (Warsaw): *SS-Hstuf.* Arno Paul
    Leichte Kav. Kol.: *SS-Ostuf.* Franz Rinner

SS-Kavallerie-Regiment 2: *SS-Stubaf.* Magill; from 10 April 1941, *SS-Staf.* Heinrich Hierthes
    Reitende Abteilung: *SS-Hstuf.* H. Schönfeldt; from 10.4.41, *SS-Stubaf.* Magill
    1.Schwadron: *SS-Hstuf.* Otto Meisterknecht
    2.Schwadron: *SS-Hstuf.* Walter Dunsch
    3.Schwadron: *SS-Hstuf.* W. Reichenwallner
    4.(MG) Schwadron: *SS-Ostuf.* Kurt Weber
    5.(IG) Schwadron: *SS-Hstuf.* H. Schönfeldt
    6.(Tec.) Schwadron: : *SS-Ustuf.* F. Maletta
    7.(Radfahr/Aufkl.)Schwadron: *SS-Ostuf.* Hampel
    8.reit.Bttr. (Warsaw): *SS-Hstuf.* F. Meyer
    Leichte Kav. Kol.: SS-Ostuf. Paul Hoppe

SS-Staf. **Heinrich Hierthes.**

A depot battalion was formed based on the two earlier squadrons, under the command of *SS-Hstuf.* Hans-Viktor von Zastrow, future commander of *SS-Kavallerie-Regiment 3*. The battalion headquarters was located first at Tarnow and later in Warsaw. *1.Ersatz-Schwadron* (Kielce) was formed based on *4.Schwadron* of *SS-Kavallerie-Regiment 1*, while *2.Ersatz-Schwadron* (Chelm) was based on *4.Schwadron* of *SS-Kavallerie-Regiment 2*. Both of these squadrons were later transferred to Warsaw. A third depot squadron was created in late March at the *SS-Hauptreitschule* in Munich. During March and April, unit training resumed at all levels. There were firing exercises, night marches, and tiring rides on horseback. New recruits also arrived to replenish the ranks of the squadrons. On April 9, the two regiments were put under the direct subordination of the *SS-FHA*.

Bibliography
Massimiliano Afiero, "*8.SS-Kavallerie-Division Florian Geyer*", Associazione Culturale Ritterkreuz
Massimiliano Afiero, "*The 8th Waffen-SS Cavalry Division Florian Geyer*", Schiffer Publishing

General der Waffen-SS
Herbert Otto Gille: a Biographical Chronology
by Michael D. Miller
with translation assistance from Gary Costello

SS-Gruppenführer **Herbert Otto Gille** (*Der Freiwillige*, Feb. 1967; Photo by Walter Frentz).

Kadett Gille, ca. 1911.

SS-Untersturmführer Gille.

Herbert Otto Wilhelm Hermann ("Papa") Gille
ᛋᛋ-Obergruppenführer und General der Waffen-SS

Born: 08.03.1897 in Gandersheim am Harz/Braunschweig.
Died: 26.12.1966 in Stemmen über Hannover/Niedersachsen (heart attack).

NSDAP-Nr.: 537.337 (Joined 01.05.1931)
SS-Nr.: 39.854 (Joined 10.10.1931)
Deutsche Heer: 01.09.1914-31.03.1919

Promotions

01.09.1914: *Fähnrich*
27.01.1915: *Leutnant*
31.03.1919: *Oberleutnant a. D.*
10.10.1931: *SS-Anwärter*
25.09.1932: *SS-Scharführer*
27.01.1933: *SS-Truppführer*
20.04.1933: *SS-Sturmführer*
20.04.1935: *SS-Obersturmführer*
09.11.1935: *SS-Hauptsturmführer*
20.04.1937: *SS-Sturmbannführer*
19.10.1939: *SS-Obersturmbannführer*
30.01.1941: *SS-Standartenführer*
01.10.1941: *SS-Oberführer*
01.12.1942: *SS-Brigadeführer und Generalmajor der Waffen-SS (mit Wirkung vom 09.11.1942)*
09.11.1943: *SS-Gruppenführer und Generalleutnant der Waffen-SS*
09.11.1944: *SS-Obergruppenführer und General der Waffen-SS*

Career

00.00.1903 - ca. 1907: *Bürgerschule* in Gandersheim.

ca. 1907 - 00.03.1909: *Gymnasium* in Braunschweig.

00.04.1909 - 00.04.1914: Entered the *Preußische Kadettenkorps*, attending the *Kadettenschule Bensburg-am-Rhein*.

SS-Ustuf. Gille during his temporary assignment to *I. Sturmbann/SS-Standarte 2/SS-Verfügungstruppen* (07.06.1934 - 14.08.1934). Note the "SS2" collar tab and "Württemberg" cuff title of the *Politische Bereitschaft* based in Ellwangen.

00.04.1914 - 00.08.1914: Attended the *Haupt-Kadettenanstalt Groß-Lichterfelde* (graduated *Obersekunda*).

10.08.1914 - 28.12.1914: Entered service as *Fähnrich*, assigned to *II. Abteilung/2. Badische Feldartillerie-Regiment Nr. 30* (Rastatt).

29.12.1914 - 24.01.1919: Assigned to *Reserve-Feldartillerie-Regiment 55* in *75. Reserve-Infanterie-Division* based at *Truppenübungsplatz Heuberg*. Assigned as *Zugführer* and *Batterieoffizier* from 27.01.1915 - 00.01.1917 and as *Führer* of *1. Batterie* from 00.01.1917 to 24.01.1919 (when the regiment was disbanded).

25.01.1919 - 31.03.1919: Assigned to *2. Badischen Feldartillerie-Regiment Nr. 30*.

31.03.1919: Discharged from active military service.

01.04.1919 - 00.00.1920: Studied agricultural administration while gaining practical experience at the estate Bätzigerode bei Cassel.

00.00.1920 - 00.00.1921: Administrator of the estate Bamhof.

00.00.1921 - 00.00.1923: Administrator of the estate Abbesbuttel (near Meine).

00.00.1922 - 00.00.1926: Member of the "Stahlhelm"-Bund.

00.00.1923 - 00.00.1925: Inspector of an estate near Immendorf (in the vicinity of Salzgitter), then (for 8 months) of the estate Bährdorf bei Oebisfelde, near Magdeburg.

00.00.1925 - Autumn 1927: Independent inspector for the private estate of Stemmen bei Hannover.

00.00.1928 - 00.00.1929: Independent inspector for the private estate of Poggenhagen bei Neustadt am Rübenberge (Steinhuder Meer).

00.00.1929 - 00.00.1931: Travelling salesman for the automotive factory *Büssing-NAG Vereinigte Nutzkraftwagen*, Braunschweig.

00.00.1931 - 00.00.1933: Self-employed businessman in the automotive field.

SS-Hauptsturmführer Gille, ca. 1936. (NARA)

SS-Stubaf. Gille, ca. 1938. (*Max Williams*)

25.01.1931: Sentenced to a 20 *Reichsmark* fine (with option of serving 4 days' jail time) for gambling.

01.05.1931: Joined the *NSDAP*.

10.10.1931: Joined the *SS*.

30.09.1932 - 27.01.1933: *Führer (m.d.F.b.)* of 5. *Sturm/I. Sturmbann/49. Standarte* (Braunschweig).

27.01.1933 - 20.04.1933: *Führer (m.d.F.b.)* of *Motorstaffel/49. SS-Standarte*.

28.02.1933 - 00.03.1933: Temporary *Führer* of 49. *SS-Standarte*. He ran this *Standarte* when its *Führer*, Friedrich Alpers, was suspended by the *Abschnitt Führer*, Berthold Maack due to political intrigue in Braunschweig. Alpers was reinstated after a short period.

20.04.1933 - 09.04.1934: *Stabsführer (m.d.W.d.G.b.)* of *SS-Abschnitt IV* (Braunschweig). Succeeded by Berthold Maack. Helmut Schöne acted as standing deputy from 12.10.1933, then officially assumed command from Gille.

20.07.1933: Degraded and expelled from the *SS* and *NSDAP* due to *"parteizersetzenden Verhaltens"* (conduct undermining to the [Nazi] Party) and detained in the Braunschweig district prison for 14 weeks (20.07.1933-27.10.1933), As a supporter of *Reichstag* Vice-President, Ernst Zörner, Gille was accused of involvement in Zörner's conspiracy against the Braunschweig *Ministerpräsident,* Dietrich Klagges. Interrogated on this matter by the *Schutzpolizei* on 09.11.1933, proceedings against him were dismissed when he declared that he was not a part of any secret circle against Dietrich Klagges). At his own request, his case was brought before a Party court on 14.02.1934. He was acquitted and readmitted to the *NSDAP* and *SS* at his original rank of *SS-Sturmführer*.

The Axis Forces

SS-Standartenführer Gille as Kommandeur of the Artillerie-Regiment in SS-Division (mot.) "Wiking", 1941. (Phil Nix)

Gille during his command of the Artillerie-Regiment of "Wiking", during the early stages of Barbarossa, Summer 1941 (NARA).

09.04.1934 - 29.05.1934: Assigned as *Führer z.b.V.* to *II. Sturmbann/49. SS-Standarte* (Goslar).

29.05.1934 - 09.11.1935: Transferred to *SS-Verfügungstruppen*, assigned as *Führer (m.d.F.b.)* of *11. Sturm/III. Sturmbann/SS-Standarte 1* (later redesignated *SS-Standarte Deutschland*"; Base: Ellwangen).

07.06.1934 -4.08.1934: Detached to *I. Sturmbann/SS-Standarte 2/SS-Verfügungstruppen*.

28.02.1935 - 07.08.1935: Attended *Kompanieführer-Lehrgang* (company commander training course) at the *Infanterieschule Döberitz*.

09.11.1935 - 01.10.1936: *Führer* of *12. Sturm/III. Sturmbann/SS-Standarte "Deutschland"* (redesignated *19. Sturm/IV. Sturmbann/ SS-Standarte "Deutschland"* when the unit expanded to four *Sturmbanne* on 01.07.1936).

01.07.1936 - 01.10.1936: *Führer* of *19.(MG-) Sturm/IV. Sturmbann/SS-Standarte "Deutschland"* (Ellwangen). This was the old *12. Sturm* renumbered; the old *III. Sturmbann* became *IV. Sturmbann* on 01.07.1936 and a new *III. Sturmbann* was formed. The old *12. Sturm* became *19. Sturm* and a new *12. Sturm* was formed under August Zehender.

01.10.1936 - 15.02.1937: Assigned as *Major im Stab* and *Stabsführer* of *SS-Standarte "Germania"*. Succeeded by Werner Dörffler-Schuband.

01.10.1936 - 25.11.1936: *Führer (m.d.F.b.) III. Sturmbann/SS-Standarte "Germania."* Appointed as temporary commander following disciplinary problems in the unit; Gille reportedly acted with prompt and unmerciful severity during his brief assignment to this post. Succeeded Karl Meyer. Succeeded by Heinrich Köppen.

October 1942: Gille receives the *Ritterkreuz* from his divisional commander, Steiner.

SS-Staf. Gille, wearing double ᛋᛋ collar tabs while commanding the *Artillerie-Regiment* of *"Wiking"* on the Eastern Front, 1942.

01.02.1937 - 01.05.1939: *Führer* of *II. Sturmbann/SS-Standarte "Germania"* (*m.d.F.b.* to 20.04.1937, then assumed permanent command). Succeeded Walter Krüger. Succeeded by Werner Dörffler-Schuband.

00.00.1937 - 00.00.1937: *Lehrgang für Stabsoffiziere* (training course for staff officers) at *Heeressportschule Wünsdorf*.

00.00.1937 - 00.00.1937: *Gasschutzlehrgang* (Gas Defense training course) in Berlin.

03.05.1938 - 12.05.1938: *Bataillon-Kommandeur Lehrgang* (battalion commander training course) at *Infanterieschule Döberitz*.

00.03.1939 - 01.06.1939: Assigned to the *Formationsstab* (formation staff) for the *SS-Artillerie-Standarte/SS-Verfügungstruppe* at *Truppenübungsplatz Munsterlager* (under *SS-Obersturmbannführer* Peter Hansen).

13.04.1939 - 16.05.1939: Attended an instructional course at the *Artillerieschule Jüterbog*.

01.06.1939 - 15.11.1940: *Kommandeur* of *I.(schwere) Sturmbann/SS-Artillerie-Standarte "V"* (later redesignated *I. Abteilung/SS-Artillerie-Regiment)/SS-Verfügungstruppe* (Jüterbog). He led this unit, attached to *Panzer-Division "Kempf"*, during the Polish Campaign in September 1939 (for which he received the 1939 claps to his World War I Iron Crosses). He also served as permanent deputy to the regiment commander, Peter Hansen, during this period. First holder of this post. Succeeded by Adolf Wunder.

15.11.1940 - 01.05.1943: *Kommandeur* of *SS-Artillerie-Regiment/SS-Division (mot.) "Germania"* (redesignated *SS-Division (mot.) "Wiking"* on 21.12.1940 and to *SS-Panzer-Grenadier-Division "Wiking"* on 09.09.1942). Regiment formed at *Truppenübungsplatz Amersfoort* in the Netherlands. Succeeded by Joachim Richter.

SS-Standartenführer Gille, wearing double ᛋᛋ collar tabs.

While in this command, Gille proved to be an apolitical soldier who led from the front. One revealing instance of this is recounted by Heinz Höhne:

> [Like Felix Steiner,] Standartenführer Gille, Steiner's Artillery Commander, was also in the Reichsführer's bad books. Gille was an entirely non-political officer who would have nothing to do with ideology. To Obersturmbannführer [Ernst] Fick, the divisional ideological observer, he growled: "Wearing of the brown shirt is not permitted in this aristocratic artillery regiment. I'll put a clean-out squad into your room." (Höhne, *The Order of the Death's Head*, p. 544, citing letter from Fick to Karl Wolff, 27.01.1942, RFSS Microfilm 38)

Although Fick reported this "disrespect" to the chief of Himmler's personal staff, Karl Wolff, Steiner ensured that there were "no reprisals against Gille for his political unorthodoxy and evident dislike of Fick, a belief that Steiner apparently shared." (Douglas Nash, *From the Realm of a Dying Sun, Volume 1*).

01.02.1942 - 20.06.1942: *Führer (m.d.F.b.)* of *SS-Infanterie-Regiment "Westland"*. Assigned to this post according to the *Dienstlaufbahn* in his *SS* personnel file, but this is not confirmed elsewhere in the file, nor in the postwar memoirs of Felix Steiner. If he did in fact hold this post, he succeeded Artur Phleps and was succeeded by Berthold Maack.

31.07.1942 - 01.05.1943: *Kommandeur* of *SS-Infanterie-Regiment "Westland"/SS-Division (mot.) "Wiking"* (redesignated *SS-Panzer-Grenadier-Regiment "Westland"* of the *SS-Panzer-Grenadier-Division "Wiking"* on 09.11.1942). Succeeded Berthold Maack. Succceded by Paul Geisler.

00.07.1942 - 00.10.1942: *Kommandeur* of *Kampfgruppe "Gille"* (made up of elements from *"Wiking"* and *13. Panzer-Division*). Involved in fighting around Rostov-on-Don; retained command of the *"Wiking" Division Artillerie-Regiment* during this period.

22.11.1942 - 08.02.1943: *Stellvertretender Führer* of *SS-Panzer-Grenadier-Division "Wiking"* (under Felix Steiner).

July 1943: A jovial *Brigadeführer* Gille as Kdr. of "*Wiking*", celebrating Jürgen Wagner's award of the *Ritterkreuz* (for his command of the Regiment "*Germania*") on the 24th of the month. Also present, at left, is August Dieckmann, Kdr. of "*Westland*". Of note, Gille does not wear his own *Ritterkreuz*, having placed it around Wagner's neck as a temporary presentation piece. (NARA, SS-Kriegsberichter Helmut Möbius photos)

SS-Brigadeführer Gille.

01.05.1943 - 06.08.1944: *Kommandeur* of 5. *SS-Panzer-Division "Wiking."* Succeeded Felix Steiner. Actually leaving the Division on 20.07.1944, he was temporarily succeeded by *SS-Standartenführer* Dr. Eduard Deisenhofer, then permanently replaced by *SS-Standartenführer* Johannes Mühlenkamp. In an evaluation of 03.06.1944, Felix Steiner (then *Kommandierender General* of III. *[Germanische] SS-Panzer-Korps*) wrote:

Purposeful and energetic personality. Calm, thoughtful, full of drive and energy. An old national socialist. A good Truppenführer who has a positive effect both educationally and in terms of training and aligns his Führerkorps according to the right criteria. An experienced practitioner with sound judgment, tried and tested and confident in divisional leadership.

Especially reliable in a crisis. A very good artilleryman with extensive experience in the field of Panzer artillery. In larger contexts, he is not always able to put aside his own interests and is then occasionally prone to unfruitful criticism. Fulfills his position as Division Commander to the maximum. Under certain conditions also suitable for a position at the next level of service.

The Commanding General.

[Signed] Steiner
SS-Obergruppenführer
und General der Waffen-SS
(*SS-Personalakte Gille*)

SS-*Brigadeführer* Gille.

In his command of *"Wiking"*, Gille had an able assistant in the form of the Division's 1.*Generalstabsoffizier* (*Ia*) (since 26.10.1942), eventual SS-*Obersturmbannführer* and *Ritterkreuzträger* Manfred Schönfelder. Douglas Nash writes:

A graduate of the Kriegsakademie's sixth general staff Lehrgang...Schönfelder was widely respected within the division, where he had been serving in one capacity or another since its inception in December 1940. Like his commander, he was also known for his calmness in moments of crisis at the front. Schönfelder and Gille made a good pair, a partnership that would endure from the time of Gille's assumption of division command until long after the war was over. Conclusive testimony to their good working relationship was demonstrated by Gille bringing Schönfelder with him from the Wiking Division to become his new corps chief of staff in August 1944. With Schönfelder to run his headquarters and take care of the planning details, Gille was free to practice the type of leadership that he knew best- leading from the front. (Nash, *From the Realm of a Dying Sun, Volume 1*)

Herbert Otto Gille as *Kommandeur* of *"Wiking"*. Of note is the Finnish Cross of Liberty 1st Class. (*Max Williams*)

16.03.1944 - 06.04.1944: *Kommandant des "Festen Platzes" Kowel.* Succeeded Erich von dem Bach, who had been evacuated due to illness on 15.03.1944. On 16.03.1944,

Gille arrived via *Fieseler Fi 156 "Storch"* in the encircled city of Kowel (northwestern Ukraine) and took command of a garrison composed mostly *Wehrmacht* troops, members of the *Deutsche Reichsbahn*, *SS-Kavallerie-Regiment 17*, as well as *SS-Polizei* and *Gendarmerie* troops. Marc Rikmenspoel writes:

Gille... organize[d] the defense of what was both an island in a swamp and a surrounded German strongpoint. Gille rallied the dejected, makeshift garrison, and energized them sufficiently to hold out until SS-Wiking and Heer armored units finally relieved the city on 5 April. (Rikmenspoel, *Waffen-SS Encyclopedia*, pp. 211-212)

From 15.03. to 06.04.1944, Gille and his ad hoc force defended an area of six square kilometers from continuous Soviet attacks. They were ultimately saved by a relief attack made by *131. Infanterie-Division*, 4. and 5. *Panzer-Divisionen*, and *Kampfgruppe Richter* comprising elements of *Wiking"* (*I. Abteilung/SS-Panzer-Regiment 5* and *III. Bataillon/SS-Panzer-Grenadier-Regiment "Germania"*). As a result of his

SS-Ostubaf. Schönfelder, Gille's right-hand man as Ia of *"Wiking"* and later *Chef des Generalstabes* of *IV.SS-Pz.Korps*. (Marc Rikmenspoel)

leadership and personal bravery, Gille became the first of only two *Waffen-SS* members to receive the Diamonds to the Knight's Cross with Oak Leaves and Swords (personally presented by Hitler on 19.04.1944).

06.08.1944 - 08.05.1945: *Kommandierender General* of *IV. SS-Panzer-Korps* (actually arrived at *Korps* HQ on 20.07.1944). Succeeded *SS-Oberführer und Oberst der Schutzpolizei* Nikolaus Heilmann (temporarily commanding after the 20.07.1944 departure of Matthias Kleinheisterkamp). A fitness report dated 31.12.1944 and signed by *Generaloberst* Walter Weiß and countersigned by *Generaloberst* Lothar Rendulic described him as an aggressive leader, hard and efficient with a very active intellect. He always maintained a cheerful mood even in the most difficult and dangerous situations, thereby providing an inspiration to those under him. In his postwar memoirs, *General der Panzertruppe a. D.* Hermann Balck gave a generally unfavorable assessment of Gille, as indicated in the following excerpts:

My chief of staff became pale when he found out that the IV. SS-Panzer-Korps was arriving. 'That is [SS-Obergruppenführer Herbert] Gille. I know him from the Cherkassy Pocket.' Gadecke then told about Gille's troublemaking and his disinclination to follow orders. When Gille reported to me he struck me as a strong, egocentric type who had no understanding of operational context and possibilities. Probably he was quite courageous. He was the type of Waffen-SS commander who as a matter of principle always resisted orders from any army officer. (H. Balck, *Order in Chaos*, p. 408)

The IV. SS-Panzer-Korps reported the total destruction of strong Russian forces and the capture of- if I remember correctly- sixty guns and assorted equipment. Unfortunately, not a single word about the destruction of this Russian force was true. .... After the end of the war General Herhudt von Rhoden told me that the destruction of [the] Russian force was a complete lie. He had been Luftwaffe liaison officer with the IV. SS-Panzer-Korps. (ibid., p. 412)

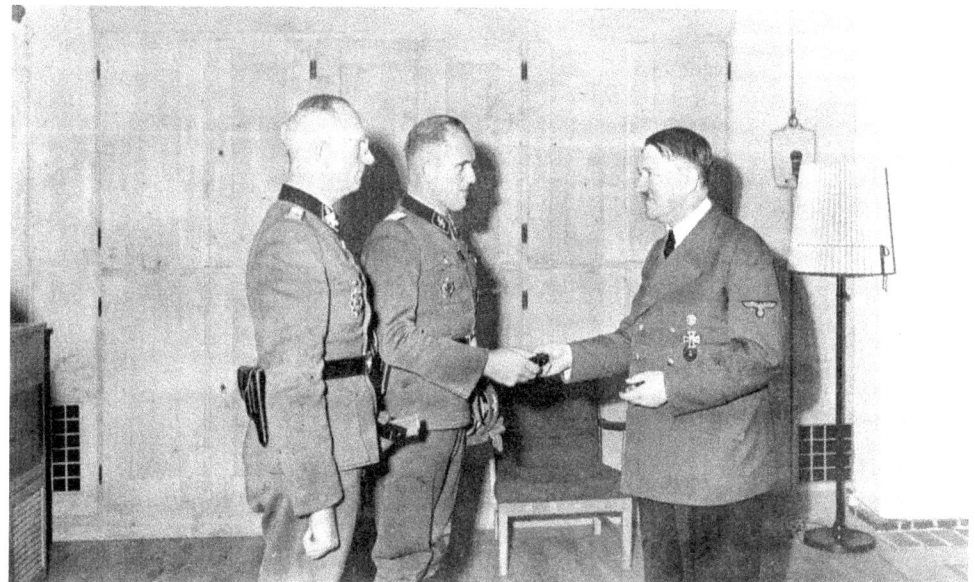

Gille and *SS-Hauptsturmführer* **Hans Dorr** (*Kdr. I. Bataillon/"Germania"*) **receive the Oak Leaves from Hitler at** *Führer* **HQ** *"Wolfsschanze"* **in Rastenburg/Ostpreußen. (NARA)**

SS-Gruf. Gille (*Rikmenspoel*).

When our offensive started on 5 March [1945] it achieved some good initial successes, but then it got stuck in the mud. By the middle of March- as I had predicted- our equipment was exhausted. From that point everything depended on the IV. SS-Panzer-Korps holding between Stuhlweißenburg and the Vértes Mountains. I frequently was forward with the Korps and I had requested relief of its command group, to include the commanding general. They were not up to [the] operational task. I could not do anything about them through performance evaluation because I could not get around Himmler's irrationality. I tried to get them relieved for health reasons. But when I found out who the incoming commanding general would have been, I put all wheels in motion to retain Gille. We would have been worse off with his replacement. What proved decisive in the end was that Gille's troops had a high level of blind trust in him, and that was capital that had to be valued highly for the coming final operation. (ibid, p. 420)

 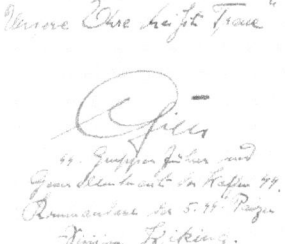

An autographed Hoffmann postcard of Gille, who has also included his full rank, assignment, and a variation of the SS motto- *"Unsere Ehre heißt Treue"* (Our Honor is Loyalty). (*Hermann Historica, Auctioneers*)

Postwar Confinement & Activities

00.05.1945 - 21.05.1948: In Allied captivity. Captured by U.S. troops at Radstadt west of Wien and initially imprisoned at Salzburg. Transferred after two weeks to Augsburg. He was later held at Dachau, the War Criminals Camp Stuttgart - Zuffenhausen (where he served as *Lagerführer* for prisoners in 1946), Sandbostel, Fallingbostel, Nürnberg (as of June 1946), and other camps until his release.

ca. 1948: Became owner/operator of a small bookstore in Stemmen/Niedersachsen.

00.04.1949: Tried by the *Entnazifizierungs - Spruchkammer* (de-Nazification court) in Hannover and sentenced to 18 months' imprisonment. This sentence was revised later that year and he was released due to the 3 years he had already served as a prisoner of war. He was placed in de-Nazification Category V (reflecting his status as a minor offender).

After 1949: Active functionary of the *Waffen-SS* veterans' organization, HIAG, and founded the *"Wiking"* Division veterans' organization *Truppenkameradschaft Wiking e.V.*

24.09.1951: With the founding of the *Verband deutscher Soldaten* (Association of German Soldiers), appointed - together with Hausser - to its *Vorläufige Präsidium* (managing committee).

Div.-Kdr. Herbert Otto Gille in his command vehicle, an Sd.Kfz. 251. (*Marc Rikmenspoel*)

00.11.1951-26.12.1966: Founder and editor of the *HIAG* news organ *Wiking Ruf* (later renamed *Der Freiwillige*).

21.02.1944: *Führer* HQ "Wolfsschanze", Rastenburg/Ostpreußen. Hitler presents the Swords to Herbert Otto Gille. Left to right: *SS-Hauptsturmführer* Léon Degrelle (*Führer* of 5. SS-Sturmbrigade "Wallonie"), Gille, Hitler, Hermann Fegelein, and Heinrich Himmler.

Following the awards ceremony, Gille chats with *Generalleutnant* Theo-Helmut Lieb (*Kommandierender General* of XXXXII. *Armee-Korps*) and Degrelle, both of whom received the Oak Leaves for their actions at Tscherkassy. At far right: *Reichspressechef* and *SS-Obergruppenführer* Dr. Otto Dietrich.

An informal portrait of *SS-Gruppenführer und Generalleutnant der Waffen-SS* **Herbert Otto Gille** after receiving the Swords, Spring 1944.

General der Infanterie **Walter Weiß**.

Decorations & Awards

19.04.1944: *Brillanten zum Ritterkreuzes des Eisernen Kreuzes* (12.) as *Div.-Kdr.* of 5. *SS-Panzer-Division "Wiking"/ LVI.Panzer-Korps/2. Armee/Heeresgruppe Mitte*, Eastern Front. *Vorschlag* dated 09.04.1944 and signed by *Korps Kom. Gen. General der Infanterie* Friedrich Hoßbach; Countersigned by *Armee OB Generaloberst* Walter Weiß, *Heeresgruppe OB Generalfeldmarschall* Ernst Busch, and on 19.04.1944 by *Reichsführer-SS* Himmler.

The Kommandierende General of the LVI. Pz. Korps telegrammed on 09.04.44:

Proposal for the presentation of the Diamonds to Generalleutnant Gille, SS-Div. Wiking. Week-long, heroic defense of the completely enclosed stronghold Kowel despite enormous supply difficulties and considerable losses against a far superior enemy only through determined leadership and enormous personal bravery by the General. Due to a particular combat situation telegrammed in advance. Written request follows.

Signed Hoßbach
General der Infanterie
und Kommandierende General LVI.Pz. Korps

SS-Gruppenführer und Generalleutnant der Waffen-SS Gille has once again distinguished himself to the highest degree through outstanding leadership and heroic commitment.

During the several weeks' long defense of the completely surrounded stronghold of Kowel, he was the soul of a unique standing resistance of a small force in relation to a far superior, ruthless, and continuously attacking enemy. His living example made the admirable struggle of the city possible. What he had shown here in great resolution and hardness as well as in superior calmness and foresight, even in the moment when the battle appeared to be almost hopeless, deserves highest recognition.

The Axis Forces

A series of photos of *SS-Gruf.* Gille in an observation post at Kowel, March/April 1944. (NARA, *SS-Kriegsberichter* Jarolim)

I therefore propose awarding the Oak Leaves with Swords and Diamonds to the Knight's Cross of the Iron Cross to this outstanding divisional commander.

[Signed] Weiß
Generaloberst und Oberbefehlshaber der 2. Armee.

Generalleutnant der Waffen SS Gille has shown superior and decisive merits in the successful perseverance of the stronghold Kowel. I endorse the awarding of the Oak Leaves with Swords and Diamonds.

[Signed] Busch.
Generalfeldmarschall
(*SS-Personalakte Gille*)

20.02.1944: *Schwerter zum Ritterkreuz des Eisernen Kreuzes* (47.) as *SS-Gruppenführer und Generalleutnant der Waffen-SS* and *Div.-Kdr.* of *5. SS-Panzer-Division "Wiking"*, Eastern Front. Immediate award, personally presented by Hitler at *Führer HQ "Wolfsschanze"* on 21.02.1944. No document in justification of the award appears in his *SS* file. Awarded for the breakout from the *"Kessel von Tscherkassy"* (Cherkassy Cauldron) which took place under his leadership.

01.11.1943: *Eichenlaub zum Ritterkreuz des Eisernen Kreuzes* (315.) as *SS-Brigadeführer und Generalmajor der Waffen-SS* and *Div.-Kdr.* of *SS-Panzer-Grenadier-Division "Wiking"*, Eastern Front. *Vorschlag* dated 30.10.1943 and signed by *Reichsführer-SS* Himmler. Personally presented by Hitler at *Führer HQ "Wolfsschanze"* on 13.11.1943.

Acts of bravery and particular leadership merits of SS-Brigadeführer und Generalmajor der Waffen SS Herbert Gille, Kommandeur of the SS-Panzergrenadierdivision Wiking, recipient of the Knight's Cross of the Iron Cross.

SS-Brigadeführer Gille has been in charge of the SS-Pz. Gren. Div. Wiking in an acting capacity since October 1942. In May he was appointed as Kommandeur of this SS-Division.

SS-Gruf. **Gille in an observation post at Kowel, March/April 1944. (NARA)**

He was awarded the Knight's Cross of the Iron Cross in the summer of 1942 as the commander of an advanced unit during the offensive action in the Caucasus

In the past battles, through the outstanding leadership of his division, SS-Brigadeführer Gille has intervened decisively many times during the fighting on the southern front.

He was characterized by confident, energetic leadership, quick, considered command, and especially by his personal example and decisive action. Often, his example of outstanding personal bravery on the front line was the decisive element in critical situations and dangerous positions.

If this division gained immortal glory in many battles, if, as a division of the Waffen-SS, it faithfully did its duty in the focal points of the fighting on the southern front under the hardest sacrifices and earned the highest recognition and respect among the comrades of the army, if it was mentioned several times in the army reports and in the press because of its aggressive, exemplary commitment, if it still defends a section of more than 25 km on the Djneper despite two years of uninterrupted action in the heaviest fighting and extensive losses, then it is primarily the merit of its commander, who led them with unwavering dedication, responsibility and loyalty, always with confidence and deliberation.

The achievements of the Division in detail, under the leadership of SS-Brigadeführer-Gille, are attached in a combat report [*Gefechtsbericht*].
(*SS-Personalakte Gille*)

The following is the *Gefechtsbericht* referenced above:

Combat report on the Action carried out by the SS-Pz.Gren.Div. Wiking led by SS-Brigadeführer und Generalmajor der Waffen SS Gille.

A.) <u>Defensive combat in the Caucasus in the area east of Alagier. Combat during the withdrawal around Alagier in the area east of Naltschik, October to the 30th of December 1942.</u>

The Axis Forces

A series of photos of Gille, with *Sturmbannführer* Franz Hack (*Kdr. III.(gepanzerte)Btl./"Germania"*) and others in an observation post at Kowel, March/April 1944. (NARA)

In these battles, the Division fought off intense assaults with tank support between Alagier and Ardon and breakout attempts by the enemy from the Caucasus valleys between Tschikola and Alagier. During these battles, due to the size of the sector, the Division deployed everybody down to the last baggage driver in the defensive action. All enemy attacks were repelled; in particular, it was not possible for him [the enemy/MdM] to break through the only supply route to the 3.Pz.Div, Tschikola - Prochladny. The deployment to a defensive line East of Naltschik in December, was carried out according to plan despite intense enemy pursuit.

B.) <u>Combat during the Winter withdrawal from the southwest of Stalingrad to Rostow. January to February 1943</u>.

Detached from the area around Naltschik, the Division was immediately deployed to the primary area of action of the 4th Panzerarmee southwest of Stalingrad. Here, following the collapse of the Romanian Army and the repulse of the German attack to relieve Stalingrad, which was led by the LVII. Panzerkorps, the enemy, making use of strong armor, motorized and mechanized forces, attempted to destroy the weak German units and to break through towards Rostow in order to cut off the retreat of the German troops in the Caucasus. Simowniki was defended against intensive attacks. From 08.01 to 13.01. defense of the Kuberle sector; during which two Russian regiments which had broken through at the rail Junction at Orliwskaja were destroyed. From 14.01 to 19.01, the Division defended the bridgehead at Proletarskanja on the Mayntsch; demolition of the Mayntsch floodgates. From 20.01 to 24.01, the Division fought a rearguard action for the 4. Panzerarmee on the west bank of the Mayntsch towards Rostow.

The Axis Forces

Gille receives the Diamonds to the Knight's Cross with Oak Leaves and Swords at Führer HQ *Wolfsschanze*. Also present: Heinrich Himmler (extreme right) and Hermann Fegelein. (NARA)

Spring 1944: Gille reading a map. (Bundesarchiv Bild 1011-090-3916-14)

Especially noteworthy here is the defense and subsequent complete destruction of the railway junction at Saalsk, the destruction of a strong enemy tank thrust towards Gigant and the hard defensive action near Jagorlykskanja. In the period between 25.01 and 29.01, the Division prevented strongest enemy breakthrough attempts towards Rostow, which were carried out by three enemy armies, in the area of Metschetinskaja and made it possible for 1. Panzerarmee to slip across the Don. In doing so, the Division was repeatedly circumvented and cut off from the rear. Nevertheless, following intense action, it was possible to withdraw to the bridgehead Bataisk between 30.01 and 04.02. It is the merit of the methodical and confident divisional commander that, in these difficult days of action, in which at times the Division had to secure a sector of over 100 km, in which it constantly fought with an open flank in which there was no other German soldier within 300 km, the difficult task was mastered. It was not possible for the enemy to break through or bypass the weak defensive front line.

The withdrawal of the German forces in the Caucasus and in the area South of the Don was hereby made possible. This is what the Oberbefehlshaber of the 4. Panzerarmee, General Hoth, said to the divisional commander SS-Brigadeführer Gille, on his departure from the formation of the army in Taganrog: "If I had not had you, then I do not know where we would stand today!" Representative of the defensive success and the commitment of the Division, is an announcement by British radio which was broadcast during the night between 13.02 and 14.02.43 and contained the following text: "When the German armies have succeeded in withdrawing from the Caucasus in an ordered manner, then this was only made possible by the SS-Division Wiking. But this division will also be destroyed."

An autographed portrait of Gille wearing all of his highest awards, including the Diamonds to the Knight's Cross. (*Hermann-Historica, Auctioneers, München*)

An informal shot of Gille in his greatcoat, ca. September 1944. (NARA)

C. Offensive and defensive action on the Donez and to the West of Charkow 18.07 -10.09.1943.

18.07 to 22.07: Offensive defensive action against the enemy bridgehead in the area around Serednij-Samodskij-Ssemenowka. It is thanks to the quick, strong intervention of the Division that following the successful enemy thrust across the Donez with massive armored forces, attempting a breakthrough at the railway line Salawjansk was thwarted by a successful counterattack.

23.07-01.08 the Division cleaned up enemy infiltrations to the southwest of Jsjum.

04.08-10.09 defensive action in the areas northwest, west, and southwest of Charkow. In doing so, the Division successfully repelled massive enemy attacks supported by numerous tanks. It prevented the enemy from breaking through in a southwesterly direction towards Charkow and into the rear of the German divisions in positions around Charkow and on the Donez. It is particularly noteworthy that this defensive action was carried out by a division that was extremely weakened both in personal and material, with a stock of tanks consisting of roughly 10-15 functioning old tanks, against a far superior enemy. Here again it is the outstanding personal merit of the divisional commander who forced the success under extreme strain of all available means, with unbending defensive will and through frequent personal intervention on the front line.

D. Withdrawal action to the Dnjepr and defensive action in the Dnjepr positions. 10/09-20.10.1943.

11.09-16.09 relocation to the Msha sector on both sides of the Walki, in the area east of Poltawa.

18.09-23.09 defensive action in the Chorol and in the area northwest of Krementschuk. 24.09 crossing over the Dnjepr near Tscherkassy. Defense of the position on the Dnjepr Northwest of Tscherkassy. During this action, especially in the Chorol sector, the Division prevented a breakthrough of strong enemy forces towards Krementschuk which had the intention of capturing the crossing there. In the Dnjepr position, all attempts by the enemy to cross to the western bank and take up positions there, which were sometimes supported by massed parachute troops, were repelled. (ibid)

Gille, holding his distinctive walking stick, in conversation with a wounded soldier.

SS-Ogruf. Gille wearing the gray leather coat of the German Navy's U-Boat service late in 1944. At left is Ostubaf. Hans Bünning, Kdr. SS-Pz.Art.Rgt.5.

08.10.1942: *Ritterkreuz des Eisernes Kreuzes* as *SS-Oberführer* and *Rgt.-Kdr.* of SS-*Artillerie-Regiment/SS-Division "Wiking"/ LVII. Panzer-Korps/17. Armee/Heeresgruppe A*, Eastern Front. *Vorschlag* dated 18.09.1942 and signed by *Div.-Kdr.* Felix Steiner.

SS-Oberführer Gille led the advance detachment [*Vorausabteilung*] of the Division since it crossed the Don and onward to the Kuban. On 28.07 it clashed with retreating enemy columns to the South of the Don near Seljonaja Rotschtscha, destroyed them and, with darkness approaching, continued with the attack towards Tawritscheski. In this way, the enemy was prevented from retreating to the south.

On 29.07 with the advance detachment, Oberführer Gille ejected strong elements of the 31st Rifle Division from neighboring positions to the south of Rakowo Tawritscheski, in severe village battles took the strongly defended and important villages of Beswodnij and Andronoff, broke through the enemy and in a bold thrust, without consideration for the strong enemy units on each side of the breakthrough, continued towards Matschetiniskaja, which, during the approaching darkness, was attacked and captured in a successful assault.

Among those captured were members of 10 different divisions of the 12th Army and parts of the headquarters who, due to the attack, had hastily fled Matschetiniskaja on the afternoon of 29.07.

On 30.07, Jegorlikskaja was taken, defensive units of the 12th Army were thwarted, rear elements of the 31st Rifle Division crushed and Sredny Jegorlyk reached by late evening.

Thereupon, the commander of a Zerstörergeschwader, Major Giesling, landed close to the advance detachment and drew particular attention to the fact that the advance detachment of the Division was far ahead of all elements of the neighboring Army (17. Armee) and that on their flank and to their rear, there were countless Russians. In the same night, the enemy attacked Sredny Jegorlyk from the west with massed infantry supported by tanks, rocket launchers and a mot. Brigade, with the intention of destroying the advance detachment. This attack was repulsed with heavy losses. The counterattack using newly introduced elements of the 14th Red Tank Corps had fallen through.

With this thrust, the advance detachment Gille aided the rearward staggered fighting east flank of the 17.Armee (125. Div.) in their advance and on the other hand made possible the safe decampment of the 13. Pz. Div., to the rear of the advance detachment Gille, eastwards towards Salek.

On 01.08, in close quarter combat, Oberführer Gille routed the 21st Motorized Rile Brigade near Belaja Glina, captured the village and advanced towards Dimitrijewka during the night.

Left, a very rare photo of Gille, perhaps the only one of its kind, in black Panzer crewman's uniform with *Obergruppenführer* insignia. (*Phil Nix*). Right, Gelsenkirchen, 16.11.1952: Gille speaks at a HIAG rally.

This bold and ruthless thrust by the advance detachment Gille, carried deep into the enemy, had therefor in the shortest period of time, advanced so close to the Kuban that it was possible for the division to reach it and cross it on 03.08.

Oberführer Gille, constantly leading from the front, was an example of momentum and drive to his troops throughout this period of combat. He demanded ruthless action deep into the night and through his personal commitment and his fervent stimulus he constantly pulled his men forward. He made the following possible:

a) the rapid advance of the neighboring Eastern flank of the 17. Armee.
b) the smooth change of course of the 13. Pz. Div. towards the East, in that he repelled the enemy forces to his front.
c) the swift taking of the Kuban.
He took the following prisoners and booty:
8283 prisoners
28 artillery pieces
18 anti-tank guns, and so on.

The Axis Forces

The first issue of *Wiking Ruf*, edited and published by Herbert Otto Gille and including his introduction on the front page. (*Author's collection*)

Due to his toughness, his purposefulness and his ruthlessness he made it possible that the operation South of the Don proceeded in such an unprecedentedly fast manner and that the Kuban was reached from the North in such an unexpectedly short time.
(ibid)

28.02.1942: *Deutsches Kreuz in Gold* as *SS-Oberführer* and *Rgt.-Kdr.* of *SS-Artillerie-Regiment/ SS-Division "Wiking"*, Eastern Front. *Vorschlag* submitted by *Div.-Kdr.* Felix Steiner. This document is not found in Gille's *SS* file.

21.11.1939: *1939 Spange zum 1914 Eisernes Kreuz I. Klasse*
26.10.1939: *1939 Spange zum 1914 Eisernes Kreuz II. Klasse*
00.00.191_: *1914 Eisernes Kreuz I. Klasse*
00.00.191_: *1914 Eisernes Kreuz II. Klasse*
00.00.191_: *Braunschweigisches Kriegsverdienstkreuz I. Klasse*
00.00.191_: *Braunschweigisches Kriegsverdienstkreuz II. Klasse*

02.09.1944: Mentioned in the *Wehrmachtbericht*:

In the defensive battle taking place northeast of Warsaw, the IV. SS-Pz.Korps under the leadership of SS-Gruppenführer Gille with the SS-Panzer-Divisionen Totenkopf and Wiking, along with attached units fromm the Heer, particularly distinguished itself by its unshakeable steadfastness and dashing counterattacks. The Korps held back the onslaught launched by portrions of three Soviet armies and a tank corps and during the period from 23 to 30 August destroyed 102 enemy tanks, 8 assault guns, 53 heavy antitank guns, and four aircraft. (Douglas Nash, *From the Realm of a Dying Sun, Volume 1: IV. SS-Panzerkorps and the Battles for Warsaw, July-November 1944*)

06.04.1944: Mentioned in the *Wehrmachtbericht*:

Under the leadership of SS-Gruppenführer and Lieutenant General of the Waffen-SS Gille, the occupation of the town of Kowel, which had been surrounded since March 17, withstood, with exemplary bravery, the weeks-long onslaught of far superior enemy forces. Units of the Heer and Waffen-SS, under the supreme command of Generaloberst Weiß and under the leadership of the Generale der Infanterie Hoßbach and Mattenklott, blew up the enemy ring around Kowel after days of fierce battles of aggression through the Pripjet Marshes in the face of unusual terrain difficulties, thus freeing their comrades from their clutches. Luftwaffe units, among them also cargo gliders, supplied the defenders despite the heaviest enemy defense and thus enabled them to endure steadfastly.

00.05.1941: *Allgemeines-Sturmabzeichen*

November 1958: Gille is decorated with the 1957 edition of the Knight's Cross with Oak Leaves, Swords, and Diamonds by *Generalmajor* a. D. Max Lemke. His original awards were taken from him following his capture by U.S. troops. On the wall above them is the symbol of the *Gemeinschaft Deutscher Ritterkreuzträger* (GdR), renamed in 1960 as the *Ordensgemeinschaft der Ritterkreuzträger* (OdR)

15.09.1942: *Medaille "Winterschlacht im Osten 1941/42"*
ca. 1939: *Medaille zur Erinnerung an den 1. Oktober 1938*
ca. 1938: *Medaille zur Erinnerung an den 13. März 1938*
ca. 1934: *Ehrenkreuz des Weltkrieges 1914-1918 mit Schwertern*
00.00.194_: *Dienstauszeichnung der NSDAP in Bronze*
00.00.194_: *SS-Dienstauszeichnungen*
00.00.193_: *Deutsches Reichssportabzeichen in Silber*
[01.12.1936]: *SA-Sportabzeichen in Silber*
[01.12.1937]: *SA-Sportabzeichen in Bronze*
[01.12.1936]: *Ehrendegen des Reichsführers-SS*
[01.12.1937]: *Totenkopfring der SS*
00.00.193_: *SS-Zivilabzeichen*
16.12.1935: *Julleuchter der SS*
00.02.1934: *Ehrenwinkel für alte Kämpfer*
00.00.191_: *Österreichische Kriegs-Verdienst-Kreuz III. Klasse*
06.03.1943: *Vapaudenristin 1. luokka (VR 1)* (Order of the Cross of Liberty 1st Class with Oak Leaves and Swords) (Finland)

Notes

* Parents:
  - Father: Hermann Gille, a factory manager.
  - Mother: Luise Gille, née Wurm.

* Religion: Lutheran (baptized 16.05.1897). Later left the church and declared himself *gottgläubig*.

* Engaged in 1927 and married on 03.01.1935 to Sophie Charlotte Mennecke (*31.12.1903 in Stemmen). One daughter (*09.10.1935) resulted from this marriage.

SS-Gruf. Gille, in his staff car, shares a laugh with *SS-Staf.* Johannes-Rudolf Mühlenkamp, before departing for division headquarters at Heidelager, 10 July 1944. On the left, Hans Flügel, newly-appointed *Adjutant* (operations officer) of *SS-Panzer Regiment 5*, seems to be in on the joke. The picture was taken by *SS-Kriegsberichter* Ernst Baumann in Kovel, Western Ukraine (NARA).

Sources

Balck, General der Panzertruppe a. D. Hermann: *Order in Chaos: The Memoirs of General of Panzer Troops Hermann Balck*, ed. and trans. by Major General David T. Zabecki, USA (Ret.) and Lieutenant Colonel Dieter J. Biedekarken, USA (Ret.). University Press of Kentucky, 2015 (originally published as *Ordnung im Chaos – Erinnerungen 1893-1948* [Biblio-Verlag, 1981]).

Höhne, Heinz: *The Order of the Death's Head*. Martin Secker & Warburg Limited, 1969.

Mehner, Kurt: *Die Waffen-SS und Polizei 1939-1945, Führung und Truppe*. Militair-Verlag Klaus D. Patzwall, 1995.

Miller, Michael D.: *Leaders of the SS & German Police, Volume 2: Reichsführer-SS – SS-Gruppenführer (Georg Ahrens to Karl Gutenberger)*. R. James Bender Publishing, 2006.

Nash, Col. Douglas (USA, Ret.): *From the Realm of a Dying Sun, Volume 1: IV. SS-Panzerkorps and the Battles for Warsaw, July-November 1944*. Casemate Publishers, 2019.

National Archives and Records Administration, College Park, Maryland: SS-Personalakte of Herbert Otto Gille. Microfilm document collection A3343SS.

Rikmenspoel, Marc J.: *Waffen-SS Encyclopedia*. Aberjona Press, 2004.

Schulz, Andreas & Zinke, Dr. Dieter: *Die Generale der Waffen-SS und der Polizei 1933-1945, Band 1 (Abraham-Gutenberger)*. Biblio-Verlag, 2003.

SS-Personalkanzlei and SS-Personalhauptamt: *Dienstaltersliste der Schutzstaffel der NSDAP, Stand vom 1. Oktober 1934*.
- *Dienstaltersliste der Schutzstaffel der NSDAP, Stand vom 1. Juli 1935*.
- *Dienstaltersliste der Schutzstaffel der NSDAP, Stand vom 1. Dezember 1936*.
- *Dienstaltersliste der Schutzstaffel der NSDAP, Stand vom 1. Dezember 1937*.
- *Dienstaltersliste der Schutzstaffel der NSDAP, Stand vom 1. Dezember 1938*.
- *Dienstaltersliste der Schutzstaffel der NSDAP, Stand vom 30. Januar 1942*.
- *Dienstaltersliste der Schutzstaffel der NSDAP, Stand vom 20. April 1942*.
- *Dienstaltersliste der Schutzstaffel der NSDAP, Stand vom 9. November 1944*.

Williams, Max: *SS Elite: The Senior Leaders of Hitler's Praetorian Guard, Volume 1 (A-J)*. Fonthill Media, 2017.

Yerger, Mark C.: *Waffen-SS Commanders: Augsberger to Kreutz*. Schiffer Military History, 1997.
- *Totenkopf. The Structure, Development and Personalities of the 3. SS-Panzer Division, Volume 1* (with Ignacio Arrondo). Helion & Co., 2015.

Hitler's Cossacks
By Sergio Volpe
part 4

A group of Kuban Cossacks, Croatia 1944.

Croatia, Summer 1944: the last orders are given during an anti-partisan operation to Cossack units. Some volunteers are wearing old German 1916 model helmets. In the background, some Italian tanks can be seen.

The creation of the Cossack cavalry corps

From the beginning of the summer of 1944, Himmler, influenced by some members of his staff, became interested in the volunteers of the East and authorized the establishment in the *Waffen SS* of units recruited in Belarus, Russia and Ukraine. Eager to increase the strength of the *Waffen SS*, he soon became interested in the Cossack units. On August 26, 1944, Pannwitz and Schultz were summoned by the *Reichsführer-SS*. The meeting took place on the night between 26 and 27, on Himmler's special train, in East Prussia. At first, Himmler developed his plans for the future of the Cossack people and his idea of relocating them on the Dnieper, as a sort of military buffer zone, to improve their defensive posture. After presenting his plans, which were very unrealistic at that time considering the military situation, Himmler laid out two more concrete issues: uniting all the Cossack units dispersed in a cavalry corps and the transfer of these units to the *Waffen SS*. The first proposal was immediately accepted by Pannwitz, while the second aroused some further consideration. But Pannwitz knew that this transfer to the *Waffen-SS* would ensure his men a better supply of modern weapons and equipment and therefore ended up accepting, but with a certain number of reservations. A compromise was eventually found: the Cossacks would not individually be members of the *Waffen-SS*, but the unit as a whole would be administratively subordinate to the *SS-FHA*, the operational command of the *Waffen-SS*.

The Axis Forces

General von Pannwitz decorates a German non-commissioned officer. Note the insignia on Pannwitz's arm, worn by members of the staff of the 1st Cossack division and then of the *XV.SS-Kosaken-Kavallerie-Korps*.

General von Pannwitz, 1944.

In reality nothing changed, the insignia and SS ranks were not adopted by the Cossacks. Pannwitz himself was promoted to the rank of *SS-Gruppenführer*, but he never wore the SS uniform and insignia. On November 4, the Cossack units were then integrated into the *XIV.SS-Kosaken-Kavallerie-Korps*, which was assigned the number XV in February 1945. As promised by Himmler, Pannwitz received important equipment, field artillery, cannons and anti-tank weapons. The *XIV.SS-Kosaken-Kavallerie-Korps* was composed of two cavalry divisions formed based on the two brigades of the 1st division, reinforced with all the units up to that time dispersed and which, after the summer of 1944, began to flow in Croatia. To this, an infantry brigade (*Plastun Brigade*) and other different units were added. It should be noted, however, that some Cossack units never reached the 15th Corps and continued to operate on the western and eastern fronts[1].

A patrol of Kuban Cossacks during an anti-partisan operation, Croatia 1944.

A cavalry unit of Terek Cossacks in Croatia, 1944.

The employment of the Cossack cavalry corps

While the formation of the cavalry corps was still in progress, the regiments of the two brigades continued their operations against the increasingly aggressive partisans of Tito. Then, starting from December 1944, they were engaged against the advanced elements of the Red Army who had arrived in the Drava valley. Between the end of September and the beginning of October, the 3rd, 5th and 6th regiments of the 2nd Division participated in an offensive organized by the *General der Infanterie* Auleb, commander of the *LXIX.Armee-Korps*, beyond the Sava. The Cossack squadrons operated in the wooded mountains of Bosnia and, along the main roads, descended towards Banja Luka to rescue a Ustasha unit surrounded in the city. Supported by a motorized formation of the *2.Panzer-Armee* and a

Ustasha unit, the Cossacks crossed the Sava and headed towards Banja Luka, passing through Gradiska and Prnjavor. The city was attacked and the surrounded Ustaše were freed. Meanwhile, the 1st Division, whose staff had moved from Nova Gradiska to Kutina, was engaged in northern Croatia.

A Cossack unit crosses a village in Bosnia, after having searched all the houses and burned some, under the frightened eyes of civilians.

Don Cossacks enter in a village in Bosnia, 1944.

During the autumn, some Cossack units collaborated for the first time with the Chetniks of Colonel Draza Mihailovitch, in the western sector of Banja Luka. At the beginning of December, with General Tolbuchin's troops starting to attack towards the Drava, with the aim of establishing the connection with Tito's troops in Croatia, the three regiments of the 2nd Cossack Brigade, reinforced by an artillery group , a pioneer battalion and other service units were directed to the sector of Koprivnica, in the Drava valley, not far from the Hungarian border. Koprivnica was reached on 10 December. On 11 December, continuing their march eastward, the Cossack regiments clashed in the Novi Grad sector with strong partisan units that also had artillery. These communist gangs were defeated and on 23 December, Klostar, a town located south-east of Djurjevad, was attacked. In all the surrounding villages, the Cossacks discovered flags to greet the arrival of the Soviet units.

Don Cossacks in a village during an anti-partisan operation in Bosnia, 1944.

A Don Cossack unit during an attack, 1944.

Meanwhile, the 133rd Soviet Infantry Division 'Stalin', reinforced by Tito elements and units of the Bulgarian army, managed to establish a bridgehead on the left bank of the Drava, 7 km west-north-west of Virovitica, near the village of Pitomaca. German and Croatian units were immediately sent to eliminate it, but without success. The 2nd Division was then called into action, comprising the 3rd Cossack Regiment of the Kuban, the 6th Cossack Regiment of the Terek and the 5th Cossack Regiment of the Don. Officially, the command was exercised by *Oberstleutnant* von Schultz, but operations on the ground were directed by Ivan Kononov. The latter decided to send the Kuban and Terek regiments on the flanks of the enemy positions and left the frontal attack to his regiment. On December 26, the three regiments launched an attack: the Soviets, well entrenched and well camouflaged, were protected by a massive barrage of artillery that immediately blocked the advance of the Cossacks. Kononov, who had followed the evolution of the situation from his armored car, decided to use all the weapons at his disposal.

A group of partisans captured at the end of the operation.

Oberstleutnant Ivan Kononov.

Knowing that his artillery and the few tanks at his disposal would be insufficient to silence the enemy guns, he summoned *Hauptmann* Orlov, another former Red Army officer, giving him the order to organize a raid to destroy the battery. At the head of a squadron, Orlov moved to the Soviet rear without being seen. After furious hand-to-hand combat, he came up to the enemy artillery position and destroyed all of the guns. With their sabers unsheathed, the Cossacks of the Don's 5th Regiment, then launched themselves against the Soviet positions, while the other two regiments tightened their grip on the flanks. At that point panic broke out in the ranks of the *'Stalin'* division: the men abandoned their combat posts and fled in great disorder. Taken behind by the Cossacks of the Terek and the Kuban, the Soviet units were forced to capitulate and to realize that they were facing not an elite unit of the *Wehrmacht* but of the Cossacks! Kononov took several thousand prisoners, some of whom were immediately recruited into his ranks. The Cossack losses were 312 dead and 602 wounded. The Soviets lost a few hundred men, most of whom drowned in the Drava. Following this victory, the first won against units of the Red Army, Kononov was decorated with the Iron Cross First Class. After these engagements, the 2nd Division ensured the defense of the Pitomaca-Drava-Stari Gradac-Spisic Bukovica sector.

Cossack horsemen 5th Don regiment on the Balkan front, 1944.

Cossack volunteers of the 1st Don Regiment.

Then, on January 5, 1945, on the orders of the *LXIX.Armee-Korps*, it attacked Virovitica but without success, halted by enemy artillery fire. Between 7 and 8 January 1945, the 1st Division was grouped in the Sava valley, from where it launched an attack across the Hercegovag plateau, towards Lipik and Pakrac. These operations, launched with the SS *Prinz Eugen* Division, were crowned with success and prevented Tito's units from intervening in the fighting that was taking place at the same time in the

Virovitica sector. In February 1945, Kononov assumed command of a new brigade formed from his 5th Don Regiment. Then, on 29 March, the unit was reinforced by *Kosaken-Festungs-Gren.Rgt. 360*, a unit deployed in France until the summer of 1944 and under the orders of *Oberstleutnant* von Renteln[2]. This infantry unit (*Plastun*) was integrated into the 1st Division. It was later joined with the Kononov Brigade to form a third division.

Kuban Cossacks with a medium mortar.

Kuban Cossacks with a medium mortar.

In March 1945, the Cossack cavalry corps then comprised the 1st Cavalry Division (*Oberst* Wagner) consisting of the 1st Regiment of the Don, the 2nd Regiment of Siberia and the 4th Regiment of the Kuban, the 2nd Cavalry Division (Oberst von Schultz) with the 3rd Regiment of the Kuban, the 5th Regiment of the Don and the 6th Regiment of the Terek (*Oberstleutnant* Prinz Carl zu Salm-Horstmar). A third division, under the orders of *Oberst* von Renteln, was being formed with the following units: the Kononov Brigade, the 7th and 8th Plastun Regiments. But this last division never became a reality.

Cossack volunteers of the *Fest.Gren.Rgt.360* in France in the spring of 1944. All of them carry the arm shield of the ROA, to which von Renteln's unit had already been attached, unlike the other Cossack units located in Yugoslavia.

Cossack volunteer *Fest.Gr.Rgt.360*.

At the beginning of March, the 1st Division reached the Drava valley east of Virovitica after driving out the partisans in the Papuk mountains. It established the connection with the 2nd Division in Suhopolje. The general staff of the Cossack corps settled in Slatina. Pannwitz was given the mission to ensure control of the Drava valley to the north and to counter the Tito bands in the Papuk mountains. Also during the month of March, the 4th Kuban Regiment was engaged alongside the *11. Luftwaffe-Feld-Division*, in the sector of the *LXXXI.Armee-Korps*, to help establish and support a diversionary bridgehead on the Drava in Valpovo. This operation was part of the counter-offensive launched on 9 March in Hungary in the sector of Lake Balaton by the *6.Armee* and the *6.SS-Pz.Armee*.

The Axis Forces

Oberstleutnant **Prinz Carl zu Salm-Horstmar.**

Von Pannwitz *'Feldataman'*.

In the night between 22 and 23 March, the Cossacks of the first group, under the orders of *Hauptmann* Mach, carried out their first and last cavalry charge against a Bulgarian artillery position, neutralizing its guns and taking about 450 prisoners.

Between the end of March and the beginning of April, the Cossack cavalry corps, still located in the Drava valley, had to face the pressure of the Red Army and the Communist bands. It was in this period that the delegates of all the regiments of the Cossack cavalry corps elected Pannwitz *'Feldataman'*, i.e. head of all Cossack units. This supreme function, occupied since the 18th century by the heir to the imperial throne, remained vacant after the disappearance of Prince Alexis, assassinated with Tsar Nicholas II and his entire family in 1918. A grandiose ceremony was organized.

Immediately after his election, Pannwitz decided to send Kononov, who was promoted to *Generalmajor* on 1 April 1945, to Prague, to meet General Vlassov and propose the integration of the Cossack cavalry corps into his Russian Liberation Army (ROA). Kononov's choice for this mission was judged to be very important by Pannwitz who hoped to free the Cossack units from German control and give him a better image in the eyes of the Allies. In reality, Pannwitz had chosen Kononov, because he had served as had Vlassov in the Red Army and was the most qualified officer to succeed in this mission. In Prague, Kononov met General Vlassov, who explained to him the difficulties he had had to overcome to be recognized by the Germans and to obtain authorization to create a Russian liberation army.

General Vlassov and ROA soldiers.

When Kononov informed him of Pannwitz's desire to integrate the cavalry corps into his army, Vlassov replied: "... *too late, too late*". However, to keep up appearances, Vlassov accepted Kononov's proposal and, on April 28, 1945, the Cossack cavalry corps was officially attached to the Russian Liberation Army. On May 5, General Kononov was appointed by Vlassov, head of the Cossack corps and all Cossack troops, a command he never exercised, as the capitulation of the German forces occurred three days later and the Allies had hinted that it was out of the question for them to ally themselves with the Russian 'renegades' to fight their Soviet allies. Meanwhile in Yugoslavia, the situation for the Germans had become critical. At the end of April, when all the German forces from Albania, Dalmatia and Italy, flowed back north to try to cross into Austria, the Cossacks continued to control their areas and then in turn, began to retreat towards the British lines to escape the Communist partisans and the Soviets. The 1st Division of *Oberst* Wagner, after covering the retreat of the 2nd Division, reached the latter on the Sokolac-Koprivnica-Drava line, then tried to retreat to northern Italy. But, the capitulation of the German forces in Italy prevented this. However, it managed to continue its march along the Drava and to cross the Austrian border at Lavamund. Between 4 and 6 May, *Oberst* von Schultz's 2nd Division managed to stay on the Sokolovac-Koprivnica-Drava line, despite pressure from Tito's forces. On May 6, he retreated west on the Varazdin-Toplice-Ivanec line. On 8 May, it broke the encirclement thanks to the action of the 3rd Kuban Regiment and began to fall back towards Austria.

(To be continued)

Notes

[1] The *Kosaken-Abt.624*, deployed in France under the 1.Armee starting from October 1943. In April 1944, the unit was attached to the *III./Fest.Gren.Rgt.854*, a unit which was part of the *344. Infanterie-Division*, a division that was stationed between Arcachon and Hendaye, before being engaged in Normandy.

[2] Consisting of two battalions numbered 622 and 623, the *Kosaken-Fest.Gren.Rgt.360* was attached from April 19, 1944, to 708.Inf.Div., Starting in the Royan region. In October 1944, it was attached to the *LXIV.Armee-Korps* of the *19.Armee*, then from 22 February 1945, it was transferred to Yugoslavia.

Bibliography

Massimiliano Afiero, "*I volontari stranieri di Hitler*", Ritter edizioni
Francois de Lannoy, "*Les cosacques de Pannwitz*", Editions Heimdal
D. Littlejohn, "*Foreign Legion of the Third Reich, Vol. 4*", R. Bender Publishing
Erich Kern, "*I Cosacchi di Hitler*", Ritter edizioni

The Tankers of Mussolini
R.S.I.'s "M" Armored Group "Leonessa"
by Paolo Crippa

After the fall of Mussolini, the soldiers of the Armored Division "M" were replaced the bundles on the collar with the royal stars and were distributed gray sachets instead of the black fezzes (*Bundesarchiv*).

The two tanks arranged on the two sides of Palazzo *Wedekind*, the Roman seat of the reconstituted Fascist Party (*Paolo Crippa*).

Next to one of the two tanks, there is also a FIAT 626NM, re-used by the soldiers of the "*Leonessa*" (*Crippa*).

On September 21, 1943, faced with the collapse followed by the Armistice, a group of officers and legionaries of the 1st Legionary Armored Division "M", mostly tank crews, concentrated at the "*Mussolini*" barracks in Rome, took the resolution to rebuild the dissolved Group "*Leonessa*", with the intention of continuing the war alongside the German Armed Forces. The staff of M.V.S.N., that on September 8th had put again the red "M" and the black shirts on, refusing the Armistice, had remained on foot and was forced to look for weapons and materials in the now empty Italian barracks. In Rome, some vehicles and two M tanks, used then to guard the headquarters of the EIAR (Italian Radio) and the direction of the reborn Fascist Party in Piazza Colonna, were thus recovered at the Tiburtino Fort, headquarters and depot of the 4th Tanks Regiment[1].

On September 29, the newborn unit was transferred to the province of Brescia, to Montichiari; the men reached the north by train, along with the few vehicles recovered in Rome. Here the legionaries were subjected to an intense training cycle, while the ranks

The tanks belonged to the 3rd Armored Regiment and had arrived in Rome shortly before the Armistice to arm the IX Battalion Carri in reconstruction, at the depot of the 4th Armored Regiment.

The Leonessa's tank patrol was also completed by a disarmed Desert 43 model light truck, a vehicle built in few specimens before the Armistice. In all likelihood, even the latter had been taken from the Forte Tiburtino deposit (*Crippa*).

of the unit began to grow rich with volunteers from all over the territory of the R.S.I. and the cadres of the officers were gradually reinforced both with a good number of men from the dissolved Royal Army and, later on, with sub-lieutenants of the Officers Schools of the Republican National Guard. In Montichiari the Group Command was immediately established, together with the 1st Company, followed shortly thereafter by the 2nd Company. Meanwhile, on October 4, the commander general of the reborn M.V.S.N. General Renato Ricci, issued a statement decreeing the reconstitution of the dissolved Division M: "*I have ordered that the 1st Armored Division" M" have to be immediately reconstituted. Therefore, all officers, non-commissioned officers and legionaries already belonging to the Division itself and those wishing to be incorporated there, were invited to report to the Militia Mobilization Center closest to their residence*". The Consul General Lusana was in charge of the command of the unit, of which the Senior Cioni was the Chief of Staff. Until October 15, the "*Leonessa*" Group was commanded by the First Senior (Lieutenant Colonel) Ferdinando Tesi, who however took on an important position at the Ministry of the Economy. On that date, the command passed to the vice commander, Senior (Major) Priamo Swich, who was later promoted to Lieutenant

Colonel. Initially the unit was almost devoid of armored vehicles and, for this reason, at the end of October 1943 the General Command of G.N.R. (then again M.V.S.N.)[2] advanced the hypothesis of transforming the "*Leonessa*" into a Public Order Battalion.

Left photo, the highly decorated Lieutenant Colonel Priamo Swich, commander of the Armored Group "M" "*Leonessa*", here still in the uniform of the dissolved M.V.S.N. (*Borgatti*). Right photo, some legionaries of the "*Leonessa*" stand guard at the entrance of the Palace. The non-commissioned officer wears the gray-green uniform of the dissolved Militia, while the tank crews carry, over the combination of blue cloth for the crews of tanks, an officer belt with a shoulder strap (*Crippa*).

The pennant of the "Leonessa" Armored Group, donated by the fascist women of Montichiari to the Group before leaving for Turin (*Borgatti*).

Chief of an AB41 of the *"Leonessa"* Armored Group in the first months of the unit's life. The soldier still wears the old Militia uniform with lapel bands (in this case even a Saharan jacket) and on the helmet he painted the skull with crossbones, frieze of the unit (*Tallillo*).

"*Leonessa*" officers pose in front of an M13 tank parked in the courtyard of the "*La Marmora*" barracks in via Asti in Turin: from the left Lieutenant Lena, Lieutenant Colonel Swich, Major De Marchi, Second Lieutenant Ferrari and Lieutenant Gioni (*Venditti*).

In fact, General Ricci reported to the officers, communicating the decision to transform the "*Leonessa*" into a non-armored unit due to the lack of armored vehicles, following the fate of many other units of the Republican National Guard. Ricci pointed out that the difficult internal situation, following the disastrous September 8, made it impossible to reconstitute armored units. It was also necessary to organize units that could intervene to restore order to those areas where the phenomenon of stragglers was giving rise to forms of banditry. The determined and insistent reaction of Swich and the officers of the Group, who promised to go in search of the tanks needed, caused the commander of the GNR, moved and impressed by the firmness of these men, not to carry out the dissolution order, granting two months to form the armored unit. Thus, began an intense search and recovery activity for armored vehicles for the Group. Some officers organized an impressive information and patrol service at the tanks's depots of Norther Italy (Bologna, Vercelli, Verona, Siena in particular) and at the Ansaldo and FIAT factories to find and recover abandoned armored vehicles to be used by the Group. The results were satisfactory, were soon assembled some tanks, several trucks, fuel reserves, weapons and equipment. Many armored vehicles were also found hidden in the countryside, where they had been left by the crews that had no orders at the Armistice. Two Lieutenants, both coming from the dissolved Royal Army, Loffredo

Loffredi and Giovanni Ferraris, distinguished themselves particularly in this recovery activity. The work of fine-tuning the armored vehicles was particularly demanding and for this reason a Workshop for the Group was organized, under the supervision of Lieutenant Soncini, assisted by Lieutenant Dente, who, thanks to the tenacity of the specialists, was able to make available to the Group the vehicles in a short time, putting back in order also vehicles that were in desperate conditions.

The same group of officers facing the M13/40: in the background, to the right, a FIAT 666 truck of the Group (*Venditti*).

M13/40 tanks of the "*Leonessa*" (*Borgatti*).

At the end of December, the "*Leonessa*" could begin training on the vehicles. The staff of the Group began to grow rich with volunteers from all over the territory of the R.S.I. and the cadres of the officers were gradually reinforced both by officers from the dissolved Royal Army and, later on, by Second Lieutenants of the Officers School of the Republican National Guard. On December 15, meanwhile, the Armored Division CC.NN. "M" was officially dissolved and with it all the units that constituted it, with the exception of the Armored Group "*Leonessa*", of the XXX Black Shirts Battalion "*Montebello*" and of the

LXIII Black Shirts Battalion *"Tagliamento"*. During the period of stay in Montichiari the Group not only followed the training cycle necessary for an armored unit, but also carried out some police actions and managed to capture several British prisoners of war, who had fled the prison camps due to the state of confusion created by the Armistice.

Left photo, close up of one of the CV33 in the previous photo. The photograph allows us to appreciate the arrangement of the red M above the machine-gun position and the wagon identification on the sides of the blockhouse (Borgatti). Right photo, AS 43 Special (Armored) of the *"Leonessa"* Armored Group, photographed in the courtyard of the *"La Marmora"* barracks in Turin. The photo dates back to 1944, when the vehicles were still painted in yellow sand, on which stand the red M, positioned on the front fenders and on the sides of the blockhouse; a red M was also painted on the rear hatch of the turret (*Borgatti*).

"Leonessa" officers with their new uniform, 1944.

On February 9, 1944, finally, the *"Leonessa"* could swear allegiance to the Italian Social Republic in Piazza della Vittoria in Brescia, along with other units of the G.N.R., and, on this occasion, paraded for the first time in the streets of the city applauded by the crowd, completely motorized and with a fair number of armored vehicles. General Ricci, commander of the G.N.R., was positively impressed and, to express his satisfaction, he received a representation of legionaries and non-commissioned officers at the

General Command, declaring that he had personally verified that the Group was now fit for combat. Meanwhile, the General Command of G.N.R. planned to set up his own Division, in which to frame many autonomous units.

The AS43 pick-up truck in the protected version of the "*Leonessa*" across the streets of Turin in the spring of 1944 (*Arena*).

Another photo of the AS43 pick-up truck.

This was called the 1st Antiparachutist and Tankhunter Division of the G.N.R. "*Etna*" and the Armored Group "*Leonessa*" became part of it, moving into the employ of the newly formed Division the following August.

In a note for the Duce, dated March 1, 1944, we read that "[...] *the armored group of the GNR, of the strength of a Battalion, composed of a Tank Company, an Truck Company, an Engineers Company, is located in Montichiari in training. The instructors are German*". In fact, the Group was part of G.N.R., but it was available for use by the *Hocster SS*[3].

With the intervention of Ricci, the Group became operational. The legionaries had lulled themselves in the hope of being able to be sent to the front, but their destination was another. In fact, on March 5th the headquarters of the Group was transferred to Turin, as a reinforcement for the Provincial Command of the National Guard, and was destined to operate against the partisan bands in Piedmont. The departure of the *"Leonessa"* from Montichiari was celebrated with a moving ceremony, during which the town's fascist women offered the fighting pennant to the Group. The two Companies of the *"Leonessa"* carried out activities mainly anti-partisan in Piedmont and Lombardy.

The first public release of the Group was in Turin on May 23, 1944. In the left photo, a platoon of 9 L3 light tanks opens the parade from Piazza Carlo Felice, in front of the Porta Nuova Station. In the right photo, the CV35 tank of Captain Zerbio, commander of the Platoon (*Borgatti*).

The platoon of 9 L3s has taken Via Roma; the commander is the only one to ear the new black uniform, similar in cut to that of the German tankers (*Borgatti*).

Two M13/40 tanks follow the platoon of L light tanks as they cross piazza Carlo Felice (*Borgatti*).

In these two regions the Group established numerous small operational detachments, often equipped with only one or two armored vehicles, guaranteeing a widespread presence that allowed them to preside over the areas considered most at risk and the most important military and industrial installations. The *"Leonessa"* also participated in large-scale operations, such as the liberation of Alba, Val d'Ossola, the *"Nachtigall Operation"* in the Germanasca and Pellice Valleys. Another activity of fundamental importance carried out by the armored vehicles of the Group was the constant patrolling of the Milan-Turin motorway, a major road junction, which connected the real capital of the Social Republic with the most important industrial center in Northern Italy. Constant was the influx of new legionaries along the twenty months of the *"Leonessa"*, the youngest came from the White Flames, the newly appointed officers from the Officers School of the

G.N.R.; the staff continued to grow and, thanks to the uninterrupted recovery of armored vehicles, at the end of the war it reached the consistency of no less than four Companies, in addition to a unit seconded to the General Command of the GNR, a reinforcement to the Battalion "M *Venezia Giulia*", a Training Company in Milan, a 75/27 Gun Battery and numerous Services. Many of the volunteers who flocked to the Republican Armed Forces specifically asked to join the ranks of the Group, preferring it to the Republican National Army Divisions. Lieutenant Savoia, who owned farmland in the Mantua area, made available the products of his funds to provide for the Group's food needs.

An M13/40 tank of the Armored Group *"Leonessa"* in anti-partisan action in the Summer of 1944, probably in the Piedmont countryside. The vehicle appears painted in yellow sand (*Borgatti*).

An AB41 armored car of the "*Leonessa*", during an anti-partisan operation, Summer 1944.

In July 1944, a unit was deployed between Parma, Piacenza and the Trebbia Valley, not only to preserve the area from the attacks of the partisans, but above all to guard the oil wells of the AGIP of Montechino, which provided precious fuel, unique in Italy. The crude oil taken from the wells was transported by motor vehicles in 200-liter drums. After a stop in Piacenza the motorized column, at night, in order to avoid air strikes, on pontoons prepared by the *Wehrmacht* Genius Pioneer crossed the

Po to reach Milan, where the Oleoblitz refinery proceeded with the distillation of crude oil. Part of the fuel remained at the *"Leonessa"*, in such as to ensure the functioning of the motorcycles vehicles supplied to the Group.

An armored car AB41 of the Group *"Leonessa"* during an anti-partisan operation (*Borgatti*).

M13 and a L6 tanks of the Armored Group *"Leonessa"* of G.N.R. on July 25, 1944, in Milan, before the parade held in the city, lined up at Porta Venezia (*Arena*).

The rest went to the *Wehrmacht* and the Italian Armed Forces. On July 25, 1944, a large parade of the Republican National Guard was held in the streets of the centre of Milan, on the occasion of the first anniversary of the "coup d'état" with which Mussolini was deposed: the *"Leonessa"* sent a special Company from Turin to attend the ceremony. On this occasion, General Ricci handed over the fighting flag to the *"Leonessa"* before the parade: the "M" Armored Group *"Leonessa"* was thus the only armored unit of the Italian Social Republic to receive a war banner, consisting of a tricolor loaded by the republican eagle with lictory beam between the claws. In Piedmont, meanwhile anti-partisan actions and patrol activity continued unabated until the end of the conflict, also in support to other units of the Republican Armed Forces. In August, the *"Leonessa"* actively participated in a vast operation that led to the re-occupation of Valle d'Aosta, which remained isolated for a few months. Eight TL37 artillery tractors were found in the basement of a large hotel in Saint Vincent, with which a Light Motorized Artillery Battery was set up.

Left photo, the crews of the L3 tanks of the *"Leonessa"* saluted while they were reviewed by General Ricci. Right photo, a M13/40 tank enters Piazza Duomo in Milan, July 1944 (*Borgatti*).

The Italian and German military authorities review the units of the G.N.R. deployed before the parade (*Borgatti*).

A L3 light tanks of *"Leonessa"*, in Bassa Val Pellice, 1944.

Commander Swich was much loved by his legionaries, he aroused in everyone sympathy and security, with his natural cordiality. The Lieutenant Colonel repeatedly visited all the units of the *"Leonessa"*, even the smallest principals, accompanied by a small escort, composed of the motorcyclist Valeriano Baccinelli, the driver Albino Medagola and the faithful officer in charge, Lieutenant Domenico Lena. The selection, both physical and political, was extremely scrupulous and only those who proved capable and disciplined could remain in the Group; the ration was the same for both officers and legionaries. Those who did not have a driving license for armored vehicles followed a short course on both vehicles and armored vehicles, before being assigned to the definitive unit. In the second half of 1944, the need was felt to have a unit also in Milan and in December a Training Company and a subsidiary Workshop were organized for the restoration of the armored vehicles recovered in the Lombard city.

Left photo, an AS43 Armored Car in maintenance in the courtyard of the "*Lamarmora*" Barracks in Turin (*Borgatti*). Right photo, Colonel Giovanni Cabras, Provincial Commander of the Republican National Guard of Turin, while arriving at the place of a demonstration, in the Autumn of 1944, welcomed by the deployed units, including, on the right, "*Leonessa*" men.

Lieutenant Morandi of the "*Leonessa*" with the crew of his tank: they all wear the new dark blue cut similar to that of the German tankmen (*Borgatti*).

If only occasionally the Milan unit was employed in public order tasks in the city, instead it was his constant effort, together with the "*Leonessa*" units of Turin, to guarantee the safety of the vehicle columns, who transported food to the two big cities. An efficient fuel depot was organized in the Lombard capital with an attached fuel assignment service to the various units of the "*Leonessa*". In June of the same year, the 3rd Company of the Group was established, which was decentralized in the Piacenza area at the beginning of 1945, together with the 4th Company, with the logistical support of the Milan unit. The task of these two Companies was to oversee and defend the oil extraction plants of the Upper Emilia, plants of modest capacity, but fundamental for the fuel needs of the Group.

Group of legionaries of the "*Leonessa*". Note the "red M" on the collar of the jacket and the skull painted on the tanker's helmets.

On December 6, 1944, the Tanks Group "*Leonessa*" obtained the authorization to use the "M" honor badge and the unit changed its name to "M" "*Leonessa*" Group. This is the motivation with which the badge was given to the Group: "*Solid and proud, even in the most tragic periods of national life, participated in the tough struggle against outlaw gangs, testifying with heroism and with shed blood, the high sense of duty and sacrifice with which it is animated. It participated, both organically, both in union with other departments of the G.N.R., in many special police operations in the areas of Susa, Ivrea, Lake Maggiore. It suffered losses of Officers and Legionaries and obtained various rewards for the value of heroic acts performed by his members*".

Left photo, the Duce reviews a "*Leonessa*" training company in the "*Medici*" barracks in Milan on December 18, 1944: the vehicles were all camouflaged (*Borgatti*). Right photo, at the end of the visit, Mussolini climbed on the M15/42 of the Vice-brigadier Donati (visible in the tower), to speak to the legionaries of the G.N.R. To the right of the tank, the Captain Zerbio.

On December 18, Mussolini visited the "*Medici*" barracks of the Republican National Guard, during his three "Milanese days", reviewing a unit of the "*Leonessa*". The "*Leonessa*" continued to carry out the tasks assigned in Piedmont, Lombardy and Emilia for all the first months of 1945, even when by now the Allies were preparing to spread in the Po Valley. Meanwhile, the General Command of G.N.R. developed an operational plan to deal with the coming days of the final attack. The provisions were issued in early April to the Regional Inspectorates and Provincial Commands, through a confidential letter from General Nicchiarelli, Chief of Staff of the G.N.R., with the subject "*Zeta Requirement*". The one received from the "*Leonessa*" Command had the following content: "*The eventual withdrawal movement, when started, must be conducted on the established itinerary and subsequently continued, without stopping, up to Lecco to end in Valtellina. In Lecco you have to make arrangements with the local headquarters of G.N.R. which will indicate the location to reach. If sudden and unforeseeable emergencies make it difficult or impossible to retreat on the already planned itinerary, you can make the changes that the contingent situation will impose or advise on the prescribed routes. The essential thing is to reach the maximum number of men and the greatest possible amount of material (especially ammunition and food), the Valtellina. To achieve this essential purpose, you will have to act with maximum energy. Since it is not possible to foresee the eventual course of events and the development of the situation that could prevent me from giving you the necessary provisions, I agree, with regard to the above, the indispensable freedom of action. The instructions imparted at the time regarding the methods of withdrawal (A - timely; B - sudden) remain the same"*. At the time of the partisan insurrection, all the units of "*Leonessa*", wherever they were displaced, followed the orders given by the General Command and tried to fall back neatly into the Valtellina, even though they were unable to complete this purpose by precipitating events. The Piacenza's unit, before leaving the Emilian city, contrasted with an *M14* tank and three self-propelled 47/32 L40, the American avant-garde that on April 25, attempted to enter the city; Lieutenant Rinetti, who commanded the platoon of armored vehicles, lost his life to save his comrades during a clash that lasted for hours. The rest of the unit was able to cross the river Po on the evening of April 27, and surrendered to Cassano d'Adda (MI) to the Americans on the 30th. The Milan's unit constituted the vanguard of the column that reached Como in the morning of the 26th, with the aim of reaching the Valtellina but ended up in the hands of the partisans. Even the Battery of Bergamo tried to take itself to Como, but on the evening of April 26, it had to be divided into two columns, the first of which sustained a hard fight on the outskirts of Lecco, on Como's Lake, at the end of which the fascist officers were passed for weapons. The second column surrendered instead on the evening of April 27, in Cisano Bergamasco (BG). The unit in Turin remained in position in the city until the evening of April 28, when the republican units of the city, reunited in column, marched towards Chivasso. In Strambino Romano, near Ivrea, the fascists barricaded themselves waiting for the Allies, who arrived only on May 5, who were given prisoners, after receiving the honor of arms. Thus, ended the brief but intense history of the Armored Group "M" "*Leonessa*", which lamented 52 fallen, the last of whom was assassinated on return from prison in Pinerolo in February 1946.

Notes

[1] Lieutenant General Montagna, commander of the Militia since 17 September, stated that he had recovered forty tanks in Rome in good condition, which had been abandoned by the Italian armored troops during the fighting in the capital, following the Armistice.

[2] The Republican National Guard was officially born with the Law Decree of Duce No. 913 of December 24, 1943. It was formed by M.V.S.N. (of which the "*Leonessa*" Group was a part), by the Carabinieri and by the Italian Africa Police. The G.N.R. became part of the Republican National Army, as the first combat unit, on August 14, 1944, with Decree Law 469.

[3] Chief of SS and Police in Italy.

Bibliography

Paolo Crippa, "*The tankers of Mussolini: Armored Group "M" "Leonessa" from MVSN to RSI*", Soldiershop Publishing

German Antitank Rifles in WW2
by Massimiliano Afiero

British tanks on the attack, Western front 1917.

The first antitank weapons were fielded during the First World War to cope with the sudden advent of British tanks, which appeared on the battlefield beginning in 1916. The Germans initially thought to rely on what they already had at hand, to come up with a weapon capable of dealing with this new type of threat, without having to wait too long in developing a specific new technology. Among the six companies charged with furnishing a response to the impelling needs at the front, it was *Mauser* that came out ahead; the weapon it proposed was designated the *Tankgewehr* (or *Tankabwehrgewehr*, antitank rifle) and was based on the German *Gewehr 98* that was the standard German infantry issue rifle.

A German 13.2mm Mauser *Tankgewehr M1918* anti-tank rifle team of *Infanterie-Regiment "König Wilhelm I" Nr. 124, 27 Wurttemberg Infanterie-Division,* France 1918.

In essence, the *Mauser* technicians simply increased the caliber of the *Gewehr 98*, increasing from 7.92x57mm to 13.2x92mm, lengthening the barrel to provide sufficient power with the new caliber, and to allow the rifle to be mounted on the bipod used for the MG 08/15 machine gun as well as the bipod issued with the rifle. By doing that, it was possible for *Mauser* to begin production of the new weapon in the early months of 1918, managing to produce 15,820 pieces until the Armistice. Experience gained from the *T-Gewehr*, despite the negative outcome of the war, demonstrated the validity of the weapon as well as the basic idea, to the point that many other nations began to show great interest in the studies made by the *Mauser* technicians and began to develop their own antitank rifles.

'*Ein besonders konstruiertes Gewehr zur Bekämpfung der Tanks.*' **In English, it says: '*a specially designed rifle to combat the tanks*'. The text on the photo describes the** *Tankgewehr M1918* **or** *Mauser T-Gewehr.* **Approximately 15,800 of these rifles were produced.**

Training with a *Panzerbüchse 38.*

With the end of the conflict and the Treaty of Versailles, Germany was drastically limited with respect to weapons development and during the 1920s activity relating to antitank weapons was very limited. It was only after Hitler's rise to power, with his policy of rearmament, that this type of armament underwent a phase of rebirth.

Panzerbüchse 38

In fact, towards the end of the 1930s the *Panzerbüchse 38* (*PzB 38*) produced by the *Gustloff-Werke* of Suhl, which constituted the first example of a German rifle developed ex-novo as an antitank rifle, made its appearance. It was a rather sleek manually loaded single-shot weapon, very similar to a large rifle and fully 162 centimeters long, and rather heavy, despite the fact that it was made entirely of metal with stamped parts: it weighed 16.2 kg, that is, 4 kg more than an *MG-34*. The *PzB 38* was also fitted with a bipod, the same as that used on the *MG-34*, with a padded ergonometric buttstock to better absorb the strong recoil, and two ten-round ammunition magazines located on either side of the rifle.

The *Panzerbüchse 38* produced by *Gustloff-Werke* of Suhl.

Its performance was rather good, especially when compared to the foreign competitors of the time. The weapon was in fact capable of penetrating armor up to 25mm thick at a distance of up to 300 meters, despite the 7.92x92mm cartridge (*Patrone 318*) instead of the 13x92mm round that had been used until then by the *Tankgewehr* for antitank employment, thanks to the ability of the round to reach a muzzle velocity of 1,200 m/sec, twice that of other antitank rifles.

Russia 1942: the SS soldier on the right is armed with a *Panzerbüchse 38*.

The Axis Forces

Close-up of a *Panzerbüchse 38* with two ammunition clips.

Russia, winter 1941/42: a *Panzerbüchse 38* in action.

Russia 1942: in the background, a *Panzerbüchse 38*.

However, the *PzB 38* action was based on a unique mechanism, which was somewhat complex and which was one of the reasons for the brief lifespan of the weapon. In fact, the rifle, which loaded from the breech, fired in a manner very similar to that of an artillery piece. To better understand this similarity let us analyze how the firing cycle functioned:

1). Being a breech-loaded weapon, the projectile was inserted by the operator manually in the rear of the rifle through an opening in the breech, which was made possible by the breechblock that was arrested in the rear position (in order to allow the weapon to be loaded).

2). After the operator had armed the rifle, pushing a small lever located behind the pistol grip that allowed the bolt to slide forward and the breech to be closed, the *PzB 38* was ready to be fired.

3). Pressing the trigger caused the gun to fire, followed by its recoil. It was during this phase that the peculiar nature of the gun came into play: because the rifle generated strong recoil forces, which had they been concentrated completely onto the buttstock of the weapon would have been punishing to the gunner, the barrel recoiled nine centimeters along a short slide inside the rifle in order to lessen the recoil effect, just as happens in some artillery pieces.

A German soldier with a *Panzerbüchse 38*.

A mobile *Panzerbüchse* troop on bicycles, 1941.

A soldier of *Afrika Korps* with a *Panzerbüchse 38*.

4). As the barrel moved rearward, being attached to the breechblock, it pushed the breechblock to the rear to its initial position (as noted in Point 1 above) and, at the same time, ejected the cartridge case to the rear, thanks to the joint action of the ejector and opening of the breech.

5). The ejected cartridge case risked ending up in the face of the operator. In order to avoid that, near the area of ejection the *PzB 38* was fitted with a small circular plate covered with leather against which the spent case, was deflected from its straight-line trajectory and fell to the side of the weapon.

Thus conceived, the *PzB 38* soon demonstrated its complexity, especially during the production phase, and proved to be uncomfortable to use because of its weight and because of the fact that the risk of the expelled case striking the operator in the face was avoided only by a small piece of leather. If we also consider the fact that this rifle, in addition to its complexity, was barely used during the early months of the war because of the lack of enemy tanks to be destroyed, we can well understand why over the course of a year, from July 1939 to May 1940, no more than 1,600 examples of this weapon were produced and of those only a small portion were issued to SS units.

It became necessary to take a closer look at how the weapon worked and to come up with a simpler mechanism, without however compromising its performance.

The Axis Forces

France 1940: SS Soldiers with a *Panzerbüchse 39*.

Russia, Summer 1941: two soldiers of the *SS-Totenkopf-Division* carrying a *Panzerbüchse 39* on their shoulders.

Panzerbüchse 39

Thus, during early 1940, in time for the campaign in France, the *Waffen-SS* and, obviously, the *Wehrmacht* as well, began to be equipped with the *Panzerbüchse 39*, a simplified and improved version of the *Panzerbüchse 38*. In particular, the *Totenkopf-Division* and the *SS-Verfügungs-Division* were the first units to employ the new rifle, which was lighter, more versatile and which had performance characteristics equal to that of its predecessor.

The *Gustloff* engineers developed a weapon that was easier to carry, weighing 12,6 kg (compared to the 16.2 kg of the *PzB 38*) with a folding stock, but most of all they simplified the operating system with respect to both production as well as to its use. While retaining the 7.92x94 caliber, the single shot and the breech loading features, the recoiling barrel, which as will be recalled was designed to lessen the recoil, was abandoned.

Replacing it, in order to achieve the same effect, the weapon was fitted with the so-called muzzle brake; this was a small cylinder fitted to the muzzle and which has side vents through which the high pressure gases produced inside the rifle from firing are dispersed into the air. When these gases exit the barrel lacking a muzzle brake they generate a force opposed to the direction of the projectile and give rise to a certain amount of recoil. With the muzzle brake, instead, which acts to deflect part of the gases to the side of the muzzle, the resultant force, which is contrary to the direction of the projectile, is less, and as a consequence, so is the recoil.

The *Panzerbüchse 39*. Note the muzzle brake.

Russia, Summer 1941: a German defensive position with a *Panzerbüchse*.

Russia, Summer 1941: SS soldiers with a *Panzerbüchse*.

In addition to its operation, the weapon's performance was also improved thanks to the introduction of a tungsten bullet, which was much tougher than the steel bullet that had been used until then, in order to increase the ability to penetrate armor from 25mm to 30mm. Nevertheless, despite the quality of the design, which was confirmed among other things by the number of examples produced in a year, more than 37,000, even the *Panzerbüchse 39* had a brief lifespan as did its predecessor. In fact, by the end of 1941, these weapons began to be ineffective against Soviet tanks whose armor, in the meantime, had increased in thickness and in 1941 production of the *PzB 39* was suspended. As had happened in 1916, with the appearance of the first British tanks, Germany again found itself forced to find a new solution to deal effectively with enemy tanks, while awaiting development of a better purpose-built weapon able to be produced in large quantities: the *Panzerfaust*. This weapon, however, did not arrive until August 1943 and in the meantime Germany, with the war fully under way, found itself forced to adopt alternate avenues: initially the fallback position was to use the *Panzerbüchse 39* that had been produced up until then and which, even though obsolete, could not be cast aside.

Russia, Summer 1941: a *Panzerbüchse 39* in a field position.

A *Panzerbüchse 39* in the hands of a Greek civilian, in German service.

They were in fact able to be used to launch antitank grenades and at first demonstrated an ability to penetrate armor up to 70mm thick (*Granatbüchse 39*).

Waffen-SS Soldier armed with a *Panzerbüchse 39*.

In parallel, other arms producers dedicated themselves to developing antitank rifles based on the *PzB 39*, among which was the *Panzerbüchse M SS 41* produced in Czechoslovakia for SS units. Use was also made of much larger antitank weapons, such as the famous *Pak 35/36* and *Pak 40*, which were widely used by *Waffen SS* units as well.

The Granatbüchse 39

Italy 1943: a German defensive position with a *Panzerbüchse 39* with *Granatbüchse*.

During the span of almost a year, more than 37,000 of the *Panzerbüchse 39* had been produced. This was a not indifferent amount, which could not be wasted or cast aside. It was thus that Germany decided, on the one hand, to issue some of the rifles to second-line units or to training schools, while on the other hand, it aimed at developing an experimental design which it had been working on since the second half of 1940, and which in the early months of 1943 led to the birth of the *Granatbüchse 39*. It must be remembered, however, that the *PzB 39*, although relegated to secondary duties, was again committed to the front lines as the war began to worsen for the Germans. With a war that was increasingly compromised and as the scarcity of resources increased, the Germans were forced to dust off everything that they had set

Eastern Front, 1942: a *Panzerbüchse 39* with *Granatbüchse* in action against a Russian tank, 1941.

aside in the vain attempt to check the Allied forces on three separate fronts. During Operation *Market Garden* for example, some training units of the *16.SS-Panzergrenadier Reichsführer*, quartered in Arnhem, made use of several *PzB 39* against the British 1st Parachute Division, proving to be very effective against the armor of the light airborne infantry support vehicles that had been landed by glider. Returning to the *Granatbüchse*

39, the idea of using a rifle to launch grenades certainly was nothing new. In fact, for some time, the Germans could count on *Mauser K98* rifles with *Schiessbecher* adapter to launch *Große Gewehrpanzergranate* type antitank grenades, capable of penetrating up to 70mm or armor at a maximum range of 100 meters.

The *Granatbüchse 39*. Note the *Schiessbecher* adapter for launching grenades mounted on the muzzle.

German unit on the Eastern Front, Summer 1941: the soldier on the left, is carrying a *Panzerbüchse 39*.

The same principle, applied to the *Panzerbücshe 39*, gave rise to the *Granatbüchse 39*, which was nothing more than a *PzB 39*, but lighter (10.5 kg) and shorter (123 cm), equipped with a *Schiessbecher* grenade launcher and *Patrone 318* blank ammunition. Compared to a *Mauser 98K* with a grenade launcher, the *Granatbüchse 39* had a greater range and greater accuracy thanks to the presence of its bipod. Nevertheless, its late entry into service, which occurred in early 1943, ended up making the weapon almost useless, as only a few months later the long-awaited *Panzerfaust* made its appearance. In addition, despite its better performance compared to that of the *Mauser 98K*, the *Granatbüchse 39* was still an antitank weapon and as such was heavier to carry and less easy to use; consequently, inasmuch as the penetrating ability depended more on the grenade than on the weapon used to launch it, it is obvious that the *Mauser 98K* was preferred over the more unwieldly *Granatbüchse 39*.

Grosse Panzergranate 46 (left), *Grosse Panzergranate 61* (right).

A German soldier with *Panzerbüchse 39* on Eastern Front, 1941.

These two factors, the advent of the *Panzerfaust* and the lesser versatility compared to a *Mauser 98K*, were enough to definitively seal the fate of this and other antitank weapons, so much so that in October 1944, the *Heereswaffenamt* decided to suspend production of all types of antitank rifles and to concentrate all available resources on the *Panzerfaust* and *Panzerschrek*. The brief experience with the *Granatbüchse* was not completely useless. In fact, the ability to launch increasingly more powerful grenades by using issue rifles prompted the SS to pursue that avenue independently. Thanks to its control of several armaments factories in Czechoslovakia, the SS undertook separate research projects which led to two types of very powerful antitank grenades: the *SS-Gewehrpanzergranate 46* and the *SS-Gewehrpanzergranate 61*, capable, respectively, of penetrating 90mm and 125mm of armor. In addition, the SS paid particular attention to designs by *Bergmann & Co.*, developers of the MP35 submachine gun, which beginning in 1943 were working on a new type of two-stage grenade, the *Doppelschußgranate*, with high penetration ability of well over 150mm. The *SS-Gewehrpanzergranate 46, 61* and the *Doppelschußgranate* were all worthwhile designs, capable of providing excellent alternatives in the absence of the *Panzerfaust* whose production, even though impressive, was not able to keep up with wartime requirements. Unfortunately, as with other cutting-edge German designs, time was the enemy of the SS arms research and development; while the *SS-Gewehrpanzergranate 46* and *61* were able to enter production in late 1944, although in modest quantities, the *Doppelschußgranate* did not make it past the test stage and did not reach production.

Panzerbüchse M SS 41

Development of antitank rifles in Germany continued even following entry into service of the *Panzerbüchse 39*, in order to perfect a design which, initially, seemed to be the only one that could quickly guarantee positive results. However, this choice soon showed its limited prospects, due to the fact that the objective limitations of the technology used, that of the rifle, did not allow for any increased improvements in the weapon's performance, unless it was at the expense of other characteristics, such as weight, overall size or caliber.

In essence, although it was possible to increase the weapon's penetration capability, but it would have involved a step backward in terms of versatility, transportability of ease of use and at that point it would have made little sense to invest time and resources in a hybrid between a rifle and an antitank cannon.

The *PzB M SS 41* developed for the SS by *Zbrojovka* of Brno.

This was confirmed by the fact that the Germans, contemporaneously, explored other technologies (such as that of the *Panzerfaust*) and that successive development of the *Panzerbüchse 39* did not progress past the prototype phase. Nevertheless, on its own initiative and parallel to activity by the *Heereswaffenamt*, the SS decided to bet on rifle-based technology, giving rise to a design designated *Panzerbüchse M SS 41*. Being able to rely on its control of *Zbrojovka*, an armaments factory in Brno, Czechoslovakia, the SS was able to develop and produce its own designs for antitank armaments. That factory was charged with developing the *Panzerbüchse M SS 41* which, by order of the SS, was to be capable of firing the *Patrone 318* (7.92x94mm) ammunition, which was being used for other German army antitank rifles. The *Zbrojovka* engineers, who before the war had been working on a *"bullpup"* type of antitank weapon, demonstrating their talent by creating a very respectable weapon which was compact (127 cm), light (12.9 kg) and with a theoretical rate of fire of seventy rounds per minute.

The weapon, both because of the desires of the SS as well as by its characteristics, was suitable for use against light armored vehicles and for use in static positions. However, neither its use nor its production was noteworthy; around a thousand were produced, which was a small number when considering that the *PzB 39* production figure was 37,000. It is likely that the *PzB M SS 41*, even though a good design, fell as a priority for the SS at the time when, once they had received their baptism of fire in 1942, new categories of armaments opened brighter horizons.

Bibliography
M. Afiero, "*SS-Panzerknacker:uomini contro carri*", Soldiershop Publishing
M. Afiero, "*Panzerknacker*", Kagero Publishing

TITOLI PUBBLICATI - ALREADY PUBLISHING

WW2 AXIS FORCES

www.ingramcontent.com/pod-product-compliance
Ingram Content Group UK Ltd.
Pitfield, Milton Keynes, MK11 3LW, UK
UKHW050416240426
12048UKWH00021B/1537